THE FIVE BIGGEST LIES BUSH TOLD US ABOUT IRAQ

THE FIVE BIGGEST
LIES
BUSH
TOLD US ABOUT
IRAQ

Christopher Scheer,
Robert Scheer, and
Lakshmi Chaudhry

A CO-PUBLICATION OF

Akashic Books
BROOKLYN

Seven Stories Press
NEW YORK

Contents

Acknowledgments

ON JUNE 27, 2003, AlterNet published Christopher Scheer's article, "The Ten Most Appalling Lies about Iraq," which was quickly passed around the Internet by many hundreds of thousands and rapidly became the most-read article on AlterNet in 2003.

With the huge response from readers it seemed a natural step to expand the article into a book. Christopher Scheer had been researching weapons of mass destruction (WMD) and other key Iraq issues while working with his father, Robert Scheer, a journalist who writes a nationally syndicated column for the *Los Angeles Times* (which also appears on AlterNet). Many of Robert's recent columns have been dedicated to Bush's lies, which has made him a favorite target of rabid right-wingers like Fox TV's Bill O'Reilly.

When Christopher told his father about the book concept, Robert thought it was a great idea and agreed to work on the book. We then recruited Lakshmi Chaudhry, AlterNet's senior editor and foreign policy expert, who has been writing a daily blog on Iraq for nearly a year. This team, especially Christopher, worked night and day to produce *The Five Biggest Lies Bush Told Us About Iraq* in less than six weeks, quite an accomplishment.

Johnny Temple of Akashic Books and Dan Simon of Seven Stories Press immediately understood the importance of this undertaking and agreed to a unique publishing collaboration to get this book into the hands of many even as the debate about our nation's failed Iraq policy continues.

Thanks goes to the funders of AlterNet, the hundreds of readers who donated cash to help make the book happen, and to the AlterNet editorial team, particularly O. J. Pahati, Tai Moses, and Darci Andresen, who have kept things running smoothly as the book was produced.

Special thanks to researcher J. A. Savage, a respected journalist on the energy beat who took a break from exposing safety hazards in the nuclear power industry to jump in and make a valuable contribution to the project.

Thanks also to the board members and staff of the Independent Media Institute (IMI), AlterNet's organizational parent, as well to www.WireTapMag.org, AlterNet's youth partner, and to www.spinproject.org, an IMI communication and training project.

Finally, appreciation goes to producer/director Robert Greenwald for his support and the collaboration of this book with his powerful film: *Uncovered: The Truth About the War in Iraq*. For more information go to: www.truthuncovered.com

Don Hazen
Executive Editor, AlterNet
Executive Director, Independent Media Institute
November 2003

Introduction

WHAT FOLLOWS IS a detailed deconstruction of the premeditated and comprehensive campaign of lies, half-truths, and willful distortions mounted by the Bush administration in support of what even its proponents believed was a high-risk policy of invading, occupying, reconstructing, and "democratizing" the troubled Mideast nation of Iraq. As we shall see, nearly every major assertion of our government in arguing for the conquest of Iraq has proved false and led us to the deadly, painful, and expensive mess in which we and the Iraqi people are now stuck, possibly for years or even decades to come.

Yet, while the White House's case for war, hatched long before the devastating attacks of September 11, 2001, has been unraveling steadily since it first was made public, the president is not only free of the inconvenience of impeachment proceedings inflicted on his predecessor for lying about a sexual peccadillo, but rather stands unbowed, with excellent chances of winning the next election. This, despite the fact he has overseen a stagnant economy and created a soaring federal deficit.

Why? One possible answer is that many Americans, legitimately shaken by 9/11, still believe that during this extraordinary period the ends *do* justify the means and are willing to trust the president when he says remaking Iraq will make us safer. Others are cynical and think that since "all politicians lie," the Bush administration's aversion to telling the truth is just "par for the course."

9

We hope this book will help to wake many to the reality of our country's Iraq policy: It was formulated by a small group of influential radicals who dominate the Bush administration's foreign policy; 9/11 was exploited by these armchair warriors to pursue their pet project; their understanding of what it would take to pacify and build a new Iraq was hopelessly arrogant and uninformed; and the resulting quagmire has cost our country the lives of hundreds of soldiers and tens of billions of dollars.

In this context of death and great loss, the lies Bush and his cabinet told us about Iraq are not the sly fibs of a debating candidate or the sins of omission of a clever press secretary. Lying about matters of war and state is a shameless abuse of power, simply inexcusable.

IN A DEMOCRACY, of course, it always matters a great deal whether or not our leaders tell the truth. From the first declarations of the Founding Fathers, it has been clear our representative system demands the independence of an informed citizenry to insure that they do. And yet, in the two years since 9/11, we have seen very little of both, as fear, lies, and jingoism have stifled the best aspects of our national nature. Our media, too, have often been cowed and lazy, shucking their constitutionally enshrined, critically important role of holding official authority accountable.

This is a role of particular importance when it comes to the power of our government to commit us to the very "foreign entanglements" that George Washington eloquently warned us against. For all its noble purpose and ultimately successful aftermath, World War II has been the exception not the rule. Vietnam was only one sorry example of the mess we make out of things—the lives lost, the budgets busted—when our leaders lie to us about their intentions or grasp of the situation.

Yet that is exactly what has happened once again in Iraq in 2003. The public was systematically deceived as to the true purposes of the war, as well as the overwhelming risks and dangers of assuming complete responsibility for a nation as large, complex, and difficult to rule as Iraq. That much of the American public bought it all, even after the main supporting "facts" of the government's case collapsed, makes it all the more alarming. We are only a democratic nation to the extent that we retain the ability and wherewithal to govern those we elect to represent us as leaders.

In the public's defense, the suffering, death, and symbolism of 9/11, a brutal surprise attack perhaps more shocking than Pearl Harbor, made us feel extremely vulnerable, physically and emotionally. It was a moment that called for strong yet responsible leadership and broad international cooperation. Instead, our president chose to make Iraq the centerpiece of a divisive and unilateral, unfocused and ill-conceived "war on terror."

The key to supporting this tenuous construction was a triangle of fear: Link Iraq's megalomaniacal dictator, Saddam Hussein, to both a vast arsenal of weapons of mass destruction he was alleged to possess and to the terrorist organization Al Qaeda, believed to be behind the 9/11 massacre. As we shall see in this book, since 9/11 the White House has never for a second stopped promoting this alleged axis of evil which is just as fantastical as that other one Bush told us exists, linking the totally disparate nations of Iran, Iraq, and North Korea.

IT IS NEVER EASY for the public, even in a democracy, to sort out arguments that rely on appeals to patriotism and national security. Not only does our brain cease to work as well when the love for God and country wash over us, but we are often denied access to the basic facts needed to make decisions because of the secrecy employed in the name of national security. In such an informational vacuum, lies can, as the expression goes, "travel half-way around the world before truth gets its pants on"— and Bush took full use of this advantage to promote a strategy controversial even inside his party.

And, yes, when we say lies, we mean *lies*. We are not here dealing with misconceptions, overblown rhetoric, government spin, political games, or any of the other euphemisms that have come to excuse official chicanery as business-as-usual. No, something far more significant occurred in the selling of the second Iraq War, and that is the notion that a total falsehood could be deliberately sold as truth without making us less democratic or free as a society.

The key assertion of this book is that for our president and his advisors, lying was at the core of a deliberate method of marketing a war they must not have believed we'd support if they told us the truth. Why would they do this? Simple: They believed establishing a "friendly" (read: *pliable*) regime in the heart of the oil-rich Arab states would exponentially expand American power, while also providing the Republican party a huge political boost and offering lucrative profit opportunities for the corporate interests that have supported their careers and campaigns.

Perhaps, as many historians believe, the United States stumbled into the Vietnam quagmire over three presidencies; when it comes to this Iraq War, however, we were led by the nose by a White House that left nothing to chance on the road to Baghdad—but apparently forgot to drop some crumbs so we could find our way home again, leaving everything to chance when it came to pacification, reconstruction, or an exit strategy. It is still early, in historical terms, but a half year after the United States' unmatched military stormed Iraq's cities, the situation looks like a classic Pyrrhic victory and may prove to be one of the great disasters of U.S. foreign policy. Not the least because of the denigration of the democratic ideal in the eyes of a watching world as our ostensibly free populace uncritically accepts the lies of our government.

The good news is that this tragedy, in turn, has given truth, now fully clothed and gaining speed, a chance to catch up. Our leaders thought they could lie and get away with it because they blithely assumed that if they delivered a "happy ending" to the world their crimes would be dismissed as historical footnotes, quickly forgotten. Unfortunately, once leaders in a democracy begin lying and get away with it, it is impossible for democracy to work effectively, and happy endings, whether at home or abroad, become increasingly unlikely.

Another trap is to be unable to admit a mistake and begin correcting it. Many politicians, even those who opposed the war, now admonish us that since we are "over there" we must "finish the job"—regardless of the cost in lives and dollars. This brand of false pride and muddled thinking led to a decade of misery in Vietnam—including literally millions of additional deaths—and could do the same again. The question isn't how many men or how much materiel we need to "finish the job," but rather what job are we finishing and for what purpose? Until we understand why we are really in Iraq, we are likely to keep making terrible mistakes there, and elsewhere.

It is the hope here that we are not yet so committed to policies built on deception and ego that our course cannot be altered. If one lie can lead to another, and Iraq to other indefensible aggressions all acceptable to a public lulled by the siren songs of patriotism, then we, with all of our unchallenged might, are headed to true disaster. But it is the optimism of this work—and that being done by a great many citizen activists and public truth-tellers—that the lies of the administration are being exposed and that the public is beginning to respond as the nation's founders would have expected them to: with persistent questions and passionate political action. In short, to behave as a free people in a free society, where honoring the pursuit of truth is the highest obligation of patriotism.

Bait and Switch

Senator Mark Dayton, of the Senate Armed Services Committee, questioning in September 2002 the urgency of invading Iraq: "What is compelling us now to make a precipitous decision and take precipitous actions?"

Defense Secretary Donald Rumsfeld: "What's different? What's different is 3,000 people were killed."

OF THE MANY FRAUDULENT arguments made in support of the United States' invasion and occupation of Iraq, this was perhaps the most perverse, phony, and cynical: Four days after 19 hijackers shattered America's sense of invulnerability, killing thousands of human beings and battering or destroying national icons in the country's two most powerful cities, the Secretary of Defense was telling the president and his assembled National Security Council that there simply weren't enough good targets to hit in Afghanistan, the rocky, medieval host country for the Al Qaeda gang believed to be behind the attacks.

Might as well go after nearby Iraq as long as the troops were over there, said Donald Rumsfeld, presumably with a straight face.

According to *Bush at War*, Bob Woodward's fly-on-the-wall book based on interviews with White House insiders, the war summit held on September 15 at Camp David saw many of the White House's leading hawks aggressively pressing the president to go to war with Iraq, whether or not it was linked to 9/11, simply because it was an easier target and one they believed should be invaded on general principles they had been formulating since not long after the last time the United States fought the armies of Saddam Hussein, in 1991.

"When the group reconvened, Rumsfeld asked, Is this the time to attack Iraq? He noted that there would be a big buildup of forces in the region and he was still deeply worried about the availability of good targets in Afghanistan," reported Woodward, who is sort of the dictation machine for the U.S. political elite. Earlier in the day, Rumsfeld's deputy, Paul Wolfowitz, had been beating on the same drum in the freewheeling discussion of what the U.S. military response to 9/11 should be:

> Wolfowitz seized the opportunity. Attacking Afghanistan would be uncertain. He worried about 100,000 American troops bogged down in mountain fighting in Afghanistan six months from then. In contrast, Iraq was a brittle, oppressive regime that might break easily. It was doable. He estimated that there was a 10 to 50 percent chance Saddam was involved in the September 11 terrorist attacks. The U.S. would have to go after Saddam at some time if the war on terrorism was to be taken seriously.

According to Woodward's account, Secretary of State Colin Powell disagreed, arguing that the Defense proposal to use 9/11 as an excuse to take out Iraq would be perceived as a case of, in his words, "bait and switch." In the end, Bush made it clear he was tired of hearing about Iraq for the time being and wanted to focus on striking Afghanistan's Taliban and Al Qaeda. (There is no mention in Woodward's book of whether or not Saudi Arabia, supplier of most of the hijackers and their funds, was even mentioned that day.)

Despite Powell's and Bush's modest caution at that early juncture, Rumsfeld, Wolfowitz, and the inveterate hawks that dominated the administration would bide their time, win over the president, and, a year and a half later, get to run individual victory laps through occupied Baghdad.

In the end, it wouldn't matter that, despite Wolfowitz's wild speculation, no evidence of any link between 9/11 and Iraq was ever produced—or that two years later the president would belatedly admit that he had no evidence of such a link. It wouldn't matter that the Afghanistan War was a military success and the Taliban and Al Qaeda were routed from the cities. It wouldn't matter that UN weapons inspectors were readmitted to Iraq and given total access to search the country for weapons of mass destruction. It wouldn't matter that valuable military, intelligence, and diplomatic capital would be spent fighting in Iraq while Al Qaeda reorganized and successfully continued to target Westerners in bloody new attacks in Africa and Asia. It wouldn't matter that most of America's key allies were opposed to a preemptive war on Iraq. Nor would it matter that on a single day 15 million people around the world protested against it.

And it wouldn't matter that we now were going to war based on sketchy intelligence, on the heels of one of the most embarrassing screw-ups in American intelligence history.

"Prior to September 11, 2001, neither the U.S. government as a whole nor the intelligence community had a comprehensive counterterrorist strategy for combating the threat posed by Osama Bin Laden," found Congress' "Joint Inquiry into Intelligence Community Activities before and after the Terrorist Attacks of September 11, 2001," released in July 2003. "Furthermore, the Director of Central Intelligence (DCI) was either unwilling or unable to marshal the full range of intelligence community resources necessary to combat the growing threat to the United States."

None of it would matter. Rumsfeld and Wolfowitz would get their war. Once the president signed on to their plan, only one thing stood in their way: American public opinion. To go to war in a democracy, leaders need at least the nominal approval of the populace.

So the White House launched a clumsy, often contradictory, yet ultimately successful marketing campaign to convince Americans that Saddam Hussein was the new Hitler, that he was a sponsor of global terror, that he possessed, or soon would possess, the means to threaten the United States with nuclear, chemical, and biological weapons, and that he was an unpopular tyrant who could easily be toppled, after which Iraqis enthusiastically would embrace a Western-style democracy installed by their liberators.

The rest, as they say, is history.

IN AUGUST 2002, Bush reportedly signed off on the Iraq war plan, and the advance marketing campaign began in earnest. And right away, the White House flashed its unnerving penchant for irresponsible doomsday speculation.

"Many of us are convinced that Saddam will acquire nuclear weapons fairly soon. Just how soon we cannot gauge," Dick Cheney told a Veterans of Foreign Wars audience on August 26, 2002. This was conveniently vague framing: Cheney didn't say who "many of us" represented, what he meant by "fairly soon," and left himself a clear out by indicting the intelligence on which he was basing his opinions as insufficient.

Whatever the state of U.S. intelligence gathering, the Bush administration's sales pitch for the Iraq War relied on public displays of classified data to an unprecedented degree, a practice that eventually would haunt the White House. Scrutiny of the record since Bush assumed office shows a clear and disturbing pattern: the manipulation of intelligence data to fit the administration's preconceived theories to support a policy based on a political agenda rather than the facts at hand. The practice, which far surpasses the usual political sleight-of-hand employed by previous administrations, was so pervasive as to alarm career intelligence analysts.

"I believe the Bush administration did not provide an accurate picture to the American people of the military threat posed by Iraq. Most of it lies with the way senior officials misused the information they were provided," said Gregory Thielmann on July 9, 2003. The former director of the State Department's Bureau of Intelligence retired in September 2002, only to reemerge as a key whistle-blower the next summer. "This administration has had a faith-based intelligence attitude: 'We know the answers—give us the intelligence to support those answers.'"

Thielmann, who had access to the classified reports that formed the basis for the U.S. case that Saddam Hussein and his WMD posed a real and immediate threat, was in a position to see how the powerful pro-war elements in the White House cherry-picked the intelligence. "They surveyed data and picked out what they liked," said Thielmann. "The whole thing was bizarre. The Secretary of Defense had this huge Defense Intelligence Agency, and he went around it."

Where Donald Rumsfeld went instead for his Iraq intelligence was to something called the Office of Special Plans that he himself had formed as a sort of personal intelligence agency. The day-to-day intelligence operations were run by ex–Cheney aide and former Navy officer William Luti, reporting to Defense Undersecretary Douglas Feith, a former Reagan official. According to the *Guardian,* the British newspaper which was the first to bring attention to the OSP, this unknown mini-agency had managed to gain enormous power in the walk-up to the war: "The ideologically driven network functioned like a shadow government, much of it off the official payroll and beyond congressional oversight. But it proved powerful enough to prevail in a struggle with the State Department and the CIA by establishing a justification for war."

The OSP amassed huge amounts of raw intelligence from "report officers" in the CIA's directorate of operations whose job it is to cull credible information from reports filed by agents around the world. Under pressure from Pentagon hawks, the officers became reluctant to discard any report, however farfetched, if it bolstered the administration's case for war. The OSP also relied heavily on information provided by the Iraqi National Congress (INC), a London-based umbrella group which in turn received millions of dollars from the United States despite being viewed by the CIA and the State Department as less than reliable. (Six months after the war, the Defense Department itself would admit as much, reporting that defectors the INC produced had little or no high-quality intelligence and that in several cases they had lied about their credentials.)

The creation of this "shadow agency" was crucial for the Iraq War proponents in the White House precisely because the real intelligence agencies were so skeptical of their assertions. A landmark investigative article was published in the *New Republic* in June 2003, written by John B. Judis and Spencer Ackerman, who uncovered through interviews with a number of intelligence sources that there was "no consensus" within the U.S. intelligence community on the level of threat posed by Saddam. Judis and Ackerman reported, "Rather, interviews with current and former intelligence officials and other experts reveal that the Bush administration culled from U.S. intelligence those assessments that supported its position and omitted those that did not. The administration ignored, and even suppressed, disagreement within the intelligence agencies and pressured the CIA to reaffirm its preferred version of the Iraqi threat."

Bush then would repeatedly deploy this misleading data to sell the war in his speeches. The warning issued by the Tower Commission, established to investigate the Iran-Contra scandal in November 1987, seemed more timely than ever: "The democratic processes . . . are subverted when intelligence is manipulated to affect decisions by elected officials and the public."

Beyond the argument that Hussein was a cruel dictator, the reality is that none of the White House's public arguments for going to war with Iraq have turned out to be based in fact. Still, that may or may not bother those in the administration who stated them so vociferously for the 18 months after 9/11. While a great many individuals chose to protest and challenge these claims, the media and Congress were so convinced or cowed by the flood of fearful warnings and patriotic appeals that they offered only token resistance to the implementation of a major war campaign and the bold takeover of a large, complex nation 10 time zones away with no cultural, political, religious, or social affinity with our own.

MANY PUNDITS HAVE speculated that the president was psychologically obsessed with "finishing what his father hadn't"—the "final" destruction of Saddam Hussein. Whether true or not, however, this is an exceptionally unconvincing explanation for why the United States sent 150,000 soldiers to occupy another country, possibly for years. The reality, to the extent that it can be pieced together at this early remove, is much more complicated, and perhaps more frightening.

From the outset, George W. Bush filled his administration with a slew of Beltway heavyweights who had been writing, thinking, and talking about occupying Iraq and remaking the Middle East by force during the eight years the GOP was locked out of the White House. With the collapse of the Soviet Bloc, these military interventionists, usually described as "neoconservatives"—Donald Rumsfeld, Dick Cheney, Paul Wolfowitz, Richard Perle, Stephen Hadley, and many others—believed that the United States, as the world's sole superpower, must exert military and economic force to ensure its continued global supremacy.

Charting the complex and astonishing rise of this small, elite, persistent, well-funded, and self-confident band of right-wing intellectuals to a position of immense influence over American foreign policy is beyond the scope of this book. It is enough to say here that for these men and the think tanks that had backed them when they were in the political wilderness, Iraq was not just one item on a foreign policy to-do list, competing with AIDS in Africa, nukes in North Korea, or trade agreements with Europe. No, along with a rising China which needed to be intimidated, the remaking of Iraq was to be the linchpin of a vision that, if forcefully put into place, would ostensibly give the United States a platform for a century of prosperity and security.

It was a surprisingly blunt vision, and best summed up by the documents produced by a neoconservative think tank called the Project for the New American Century, or PNAC, led by William Kristol. As far back as 1998, in a letter to Republican leaders signed by Rumsfeld, Wolfowitz, Elliot Abrams, Perle, and other soon-to-be employees in the Bush White House, PNAC "recommended a substantial change in the direction of U.S. policy: Instead of further, futile efforts to 'contain' Saddam, we argued that the only way to protect the United States and its allies from the threat of weapons of mass destruction was to put in place policies that would lead to the removal of Saddam and his regime from power."

By 2000, however, PNAC's position on Iraq dropped the fig leaf of a WMD threat. In a report entitled "Rebuilding America's Defenses: Strategy, Forces and Resources for a New Century," PNAC argued that taking Iraq would simply be a logical next step in the inexorable post–Cold War spread of a Pax Americana: "Indeed, the United States has for decades sought to play a more permanent role in Gulf regional security. While the unresolved conflict with Iraq provides the immediate justification, the need for a substantial American force presence in the Gulf transcends the issue of the regime of Saddam Hussein."

So, in the hours after 9/11, these guys were well-primed to spring into action. A week after 9/11, 41 neoconservative heavyweights signed a PNAC letter to Bush urging him to extend the war on terrorism to Iraq— as well as to Afghanistan, Iran, Syria, and the Palestinian Authority:

> We agree with Secretary of State Powell's recent statement that Saddam Hussein "is one of the leading terrorists on the face of the Earth. . . ." It may be that the Iraqi government provided assistance in some form to the recent attack on the United States. But even if evidence does not link Iraq directly to the attack, any strategy aiming at the eradication of terrorism and its sponsors must include a determined effort to remove Saddam Hussein from power in Iraq. Failure to undertake such an effort will constitute an early and perhaps decisive surren- der in the war on international terrorism.

It was duly noted by those who supported a more careful approach that only four of these men and women had themselves served in the military, and three of those had done their time in the reserves, like the president. "This glaring disparity between experience and rhetoric has not been lost on the military brass," Jim Lobe reported in September 9, 2002, on AlterNet. "It's pretty interesting that all the generals see it the same way, and all the others who have never fired a shot and are hot to go to war see it another," noted General Anthony Zinni, who, as chief of the U.S. Central Command in the late 1990s, had been responsible for U.S. forces in the Persian Gulf region.

The main concern of former military brass like Zinni was—and is—that an invasion will burden the military with an impossible and perhaps interminable political task. *"Do We Really Want to Occupy Iraq for the Next 30 Years?"* asked a headline on former Navy Secretary and Vietnam veteran James Webb's September 4, 2002 op-ed article in the *Washington Post.*

"Other than the flippant criticisms of our 'failure' to take Baghdad during the Persian Gulf War, one sees little discussion of an occupation of Iraq, but it is the key element of the current debate," noted Webb. "The issue before us is not simply whether the United States should end the regime of Saddam Hussein, but whether we as a nation are prepared to physically occupy territory in the Middle East for the next 30 to 50 years. Those who are pushing for a unilateral war in Iraq know full well that there is no exit strategy if we invade and stay. This reality was the genesis of a rift that goes back to the Gulf War itself, when neoconservatives were vocal in their calls for 'a MacArthurian regency in Baghdad.' Their expectation is that the United States would not only change Iraq's regime but also remain as a long-term occupation force in an attempt to reconstruct Iraqi society itself."

With Webb's history lesson in mind, it thus makes more sense that, as the *New York Times* reported just a week after the 9/11 attacks on September 19, 2001, "Some senior administration officials, led by Paul

D. Wolfowitz, Deputy Secretary of Defense, and I. Lewis Libby, chief of staff to Vice President Dick Cheney, are pressing for the earliest and broadest military campaign against not only the Osama Bin Laden network in Afghanistan, but also against other suspected terrorist bases in Iraq and in Lebanon's Bekaa region. These officials are seeking to include Iraq on the target list with the aim of toppling President Saddam Hussein, a step long advocated by conservatives who support Mr. Bush."

In fact, a decade earlier Wolfowitz and Libby had argued in draft policy statements in support of such imperialist policies as keeping global peacekeeping efforts in the hands of the United States rather than the UN; maintaining permanent U.S. bases in Saudi Arabia and Kuwait no matter what happened in Iraq; sending more troops to Southeast Asia and supporting "regime change" in China; creating a "U.S. space forces" branch of the armed forces; and considering the development of biological weapons that "can target specific genotypes [and] may transform biological warfare from the realm of terror to a politically useful tool."

Steve Perry, writing in the *Minneapolis City Pages* on July 30, 2003, described this history well. "The Bush administration's foreign policy plan was not based on September 11, or terrorism; those events only brought to the forefront a radical plan for U.S. control of the post–Cold War world that had been taking shape since the closing days of the first Bush presidency. Back then a small claque of planners, led by Wolfowitz, generated a draft document known as Defense Planning Guidance, which envisioned a U.S. that took advantage of its lone-superpower status to consolidate American control of the world both militarily and economically, to the point where no other nation could ever reasonably hope to challenge the U.S. Toward that end it envisioned what we now call 'preemptive' wars waged to reset the geopolitical table."

In this context, it is hardly an exaggeration to say that for the neoconservatives who dominated Bush's National Security Council, Iraq was, in their minds, only the beginning of a new century of American military, economic, and political domination of the world. This was not to be a new British Raj, mind you, and nobody was suggesting we take this globocop role so seriously as to send troops to end civil wars or unseat dictators in central Africa. But in the name of spreading capitalism, Western-style democracy, and keeping the peace, the goal was to make sure American supremacy could not be in any way challenged, even by our allies. It was supposed to be a win-win situation, but so far the rest of the world doesn't see it that way.

GEORGE W. BUSH's stated strategy of leadership is to surround himself with men who are smarter and better informed than he is, let them air things out, and then go with the argument he decides has won the day. To this end, he did keep a few other viewpoints—still firmly on the conservative spectrum, mind you—around his National Security Council table.

For example, Secretary of State Colin Powell was a more traditional conservative along the lines of Bush's father, while George Tenet, the head of the Central Intelligence Agency under Clinton and a man who by many accounts was obsessed with the threat of Osama Bin Laden, was also retained by the new administration.

Powell was so outnumbered and outflanked by the neoconservatives, however, that it became a staple joke of late-night talk show monologues. For his part, Tenet, as we shall see, proved to be only too willing to bend his opinions and surrender his independence when pressured by the White House. National Security Advisor Condoleezza Rice, meanwhile, was something of a political enigma.

"Condi is absolutely the key swing vote apart from Bush himself," said the neoconservative publisher William Kristol. "She's moved over to our side. My view is she's a Scowcroft protégé who's educated herself." Kristol was referring to establishment national security heavyweight Brent Scowcroft, who was quite concerned about the neoconservatives' brand of adventurism—as he expressed in an op-ed in the *Wall Street Journal* on August 15, 2002.

"We need to analyze the relationship between Iraq and our other pressing priorities—notably the war on terrorism—as well as the best strategy and tactics available were we to move to change the regime in Baghdad," wrote the former National Security Advisor for two Republican presidents. "Our preeminent security priority—underscored repeatedly by the president—is the war on terrorism. An attack on Iraq at this time would seriously jeopardize, if not destroy, the global counterterrorist campaign we have undertaken."

In fact, there were veteran observers of Washington who believed that beyond the traditional and tendentious rivalry between Powell's State Department and Rumsfeld's Defense Department, a battle for the soul of America's foreign policy was being fought by the protégés of Brent Scowcroft and Richard Perle, then head of the Pentagon's Defense Policy Board.

"Each day, President Bush finds himself drawn further into a blood feud between implacable foes," wrote the *Washington Post's* Dana Milbank on May 14, 2002. "Arafat-Sharon? India-Pakistan? CNN-Fox? Nope. Scowcroft-Perle."

It was a battle that the neoconservatives would win. Their victory was reflected in the radical new national security doctrine introduced, formalized, and approved by Bush in September 2002. "The National Security Strategy of the United States of America" was a bold and blunt defense of the United States government's supposed right and responsibility to act as the world's policeman: "Given the goals of rogue states and terrorists, the United States can no longer solely rely on a reactive posture as we have in the past. The inability to deter a potential attacker, the immediacy of today's threats, and the magnitude of potential harm that could be caused by our adversaries' choice of weapons, do not permit that option. We cannot let our enemies strike first." The Bush administration was now free to use preemptive wars as a basic tool of its foreign policy, specifically in Iraq.

When Bush was made president by the Supreme Court's controversial decision, Iraq was much, much higher on his foreign policy agenda than it had been under Clinton. It was also much higher on the administration's priority list than defanging Al Qaeda and Osama Bin Laden.

By the time of Bush's inauguration, Al Qaeda had been blamed for a series of daring, successful, and exceedingly bloody attacks on U.S. interests in Africa, Saudi Arabia, and Yemen, including the near-sinking of a U.S. warship just weeks earlier. Clinton's public response to these attacks—a battery of cruise missiles sent into Afghanistan and Sudan at alleged Al Qaeda hideouts, for example—was widely perceived in hindsight as ineffective, weak, perhaps even as a joke by Bin Laden and his sympathizers. (Republican leaders and conservative pundits went further, accusing Clinton of using the attack to deflect attention from a threat they seemed to have found far greater to the nation's security—the president's affair with Monica Lewinsky.)

Yet for Tenet, Al Qaeda was no joke, and there had been more, at least on paper, to Clinton's terrorism policy than just the missile barrage, including various aggressive attempts at disrupting the group that stopped short of assassination.

On October 12, 2000, the USS Cole warship was successfully attacked in a port in Yemen by what were believed to be Al Qaeda forces, and 17 American servicemen were killed. In response, according to *Time,* the Clinton administration's point man on terrorism, Richard Clarke, drew up a blueprint a year before 9/11 for a concerted and prolonged war against Al Qaeda in Afghanistan and elsewhere. Clarke's plan, presented to his superiors on December 8, spelled out, in the words of one Bush official talking to *Time* in August 2002, "everything we've done since 9/11."

With less than a month left in office, however, the Clinton administration decided it wouldn't be wise to launch a war during the transition period. Clinton's National Security Advisor Sandy Berger says he organized a series of very detailed security briefings for the incoming Bush team, and personally told Rice in a transition briefing, "I believe that the

Bush administration will spend more time on terrorism generally, and on Al Qaeda specifically, than any other subject."

Even so, "The proposals Clarke developed in the winter of 2000–01 were not given another hearing by top decision makers until late April, and then spent another four months making their laborious way through the bureaucracy before they were readied for approval by President Bush," reported *Time*. Yet, by the summer of 2001, "many of those in the know—the spooks, the buttoned-down bureaucrats, the law-enforcement professionals in a dozen countries—were almost frantic with worry that a major terrorist attack against American interests was imminent. It wasn't averted because 2001 saw a systematic collapse in the ability of Washington's national-security apparatus to handle the terrorist threat. The winter proposals became a victim of the transition process, turf wars, and time spent on the pet policies of new top officials."

While it is unclear whether the 9/11 attacks could have been prevented, it is important to understand that stopping Al Qaeda and deposing Hussein were *not* twin fronts on the same battlefield, and they were actually in direct conflict and remain so—for military and intelligence resources, public and international support, and even in defining who we are as a nation. The obsession of so many of Bush's foreign policy advisors with Iraq upon taking control of the reins of state made it that much more likely that we would be blindsided by Al Qaeda, with its completely different set of goals, strategies, and tactics.

AS PRESENTED TO THE American people by our president, the invasion and occupation of Iraq was an essential component of the "war on terror," itself the linchpin of the vague, impossibly broad, and hyperaggressive Bush doctrine that the president had formulated publicly in the days after 9/11.

At its root, these stratagems were supposed to make Americans safer, although Bush's language—full of John Wayne colloquialisms like "smoke 'em out" and "hunt 'em down"—often seemed much more reminiscent of the exhortations of a vengeful jihadi cleric than that of a confident and protective patriarch, as he seemed to aspire to appear. After resounding military victories in Afghanistan and Iraq, by late spring 2003, many in the White House were exuberant and willing to say off the record that the now-famous photo of Bush striding across the deck of an aircraft carrier in full *Top Gun* gear would be Exhibit #1 in the 2004 presidential campaign. As it turns out, they were celebrating too soon.

Much of what has ensued is now familiar ground for those who have been following current events, and all too obviously similar to previous colonial debacles: the confusing blend of spontaneous local opposition and disciplined guerrilla organizations, economic and political chaos, and a "checkpoint culture" of tense, dangerous engagements between foreign troops and native civilians that wears on both. Instead of making us look strong, we have exposed the limits of raw power to make history.

In his eloquent February 27, 2003 letter of resignation to Secretary of State Colin Powell, diplomat John Brady Kiesling, who had served under four presidents, made a prescient warning about what lay beneath the White House's hubris, as well as how it threatened the very United States leadership in global affairs it claimed to exemplify:

> The September 11 tragedy left us stronger than before, rallying around us a vast international coalition to cooperate for the first time in a systematic way against the threat of terrorism. But rather than take credit for those successes and build on them, this administration has chosen to make terrorism a domestic political tool, enlisting a scattered and largely defeated Al Qaeda as its bureaucratic ally. We spread disproportionate terror and confusion in the public mind, arbitrarily linking the unrelated problems of terrorism and Iraq. The result, and perhaps the motive, is to justify a vast misallocation of shrinking public wealth to the military and to weaken the safeguards that protect

American citizens from the heavy hand of government. September 11 did not do as much damage to the fabric of American society as we seem determined to do to ourselves . . .

We are straining beyond its limits an international system we built with such toil and treasure, a web of laws, treaties, organizations, and shared values that sets limits on our foes far more effectively than it ever constrained America's ability to defend its interests.

This war was no gimme, however. There was considerable resistance outside of Washington to go to war without the cloak of United Nations cooperation and/or a broad coalition of real allies. And, as we have seen, even some powerful figures inside the Beltway, such as Scowcroft and Zinni, were publicly opposed to it.

To steer the United States into a preemptive war with a country 6,000 miles away, the Bush administration had to establish five key "facts" in the public's mind as a precursor to deploying hundreds of thousands of troops and spending billions of dollars in the effort:

1. Iraq had something to do with 9/11 and/or Al Qaeda.

2. Iraq illegally possessed chemical and biological weapons which were a threat to the United States and/or its allies.

3. Iraq was fast pursuing and might even already possess the means to build and deliver a nuclear bomb.

4. Occupying Iraq would not only be a "cakewalk," but we would also find in the aftermath a nation full of people who would welcome us and cooperate fully in the rebuilding of their country.

5. Iraq was a nation which, with U.S. aid and guidance, could within a short time become a democratic model for the rest of the region.

These five lies were hardly arbitrary, but chosen with a clear under-standing of what it takes to overcome the innate isolationism of Americans. To wage war, the American public needs to feel an immedi-ate sense of clear and present danger, be it Pearl Harbor or the menac-ing presence of Soviet nuclear weapons placed in Cuba. We are poorly educated about the world beyond, but have an innate grasp of power relationships, understanding that if you can't hurt us we don't have to think much about you.

The fact that Iraq holds under its dry soil the world's second largest oil reserves only complicated the pitch for occupation: Americans don't like to think of themselves as imperialists, getting their hands dirty to secure wealth. Thanks to our history as a former colony, U.S. foreign policy has always been clothed in the rhetoric of moral exceptional-ism—the idea that wars must be undertaken at least partly for the greater good of humanity.

The larger vision behind the invasion of Iraq—as the first step toward the creation of a new American empire—was unlikely to win a ringing endorsement from a nation that likes to think of itself always as the "good guy in the white hat." Despite Saddam's many excesses, most Americans wouldn't have minded if Saddam Hussein were to be overthrown, choke on a pretzel, or be stoned for adultery—and all Iraq's oil siphoned into the Great Lakes, for that matter—but they were damned unlikely to want to risk American lives to accomplish any of it.

And then, after the unbelievable horror of 9/11, shocked out of our post–Cold War illusion of omnipotence, Americans—whether liberal or conservative—sought security, revenge, and reaffirmation of our long-held belief that we are the world's beacon of light. Faced with these strong and often conflicting emotions, the White House offered a simple panacea: an open-ended "war on terror," posed as a new "crusade" to wreak havoc on America's enemies and anybody who would harbor them.

U.S. presidents know that to sell a war to the American people, they need at least two basic ingredients: self-defense and moral duty. In terrorism, the Bush administration found the perfect enemy—shadowy, insubstantial, and infinitely malleable to interpretation. In his 2002 State of the Union speech, flushed with the resounding victory in Afghanistan, Bush proclaimed:

"Thousands of dangerous killers, schooled in the methods of murder, often supported by outlaw regimes, are now spread throughout the world like ticking time bombs, set to go off without warning. . . . These enemies view the entire world as a battlefield, and we must pursue them wherever they are. So long as training camps operate, so long as nations harbor terrorists, freedom is at risk and America and our allies must not, and will not, allow it."

Forget the Taliban. It was now time for a full-blown "axis of evil," a wish list of targets that could be picked off one by one in this unending war; unfortunately for Saddam, Iraq was #1. Over the coming year, the Bush administration would persistently work to convince the American public that: one, Saddam has already attacked the United States through his connections with Al Qaeda; and two, he could and would do so again using biological and chemical weapons or, if we were to waste any more time, a nuclear bomb.

In chapters two, three, and four, we deconstruct each of these myths—Saddam's link to Al Qaeda, his threatening stash of bio-chemical weapons, and his nuclear weapons program—in detail. As these chapters reveal, the Bush administration did not have good evidence to support its allegations. It instead combined vague assertions, outright falsehoods, and exaggerated rhetoric that were repeated over and over again until they were established as "facts" in the public debate.

While establishing Saddam's credentials as a terrorist required "imaginative" uses of intelligence, the moral card was much easier to play in the post-9/11 era. The national tragedy brought out the uglier side of American exceptionalism: the need to objectify entire nations as "evil." Whatever the motives for war, Americans have always needed to believe in their righteousness in waging it.

Like many presidents before him and since, John F. Kennedy had spoken to this sense of manifest destiny when he promised in his inaugural speech that Americans would "pay any price, bear any burden, meet any hardship, support any friend, oppose any foe, to assure the survival and the success of liberty" in the battle against the Soviet Union. Later, Ronald Reagan would indelibly depict Moscow as the seat of an "Evil Empire," and it is surely not coincidental that the words "evil" and "evil-doers," employed vaguely to define all those who would hurt "freedom," have become the hallmark of the second President Bush.

It hardly required a leap of faith in this political climate fraught with self-righteousness to believe that not only was Saddam the reincarnation of Hitler, but that his ouster would result in a free and prosperous Iraq. Apart from the now infamous "16 words" about Iraq's alleged attempt to buy uranium, Bush's State of the Union speech delivered two months before the war also contained "a message for the brave and oppressed people of Iraq: Your enemy is not surrounding your country—your enemy is ruling your country. And the day he and his regime are removed from power will be the day of your liberation."

If the looming threat of bomb-dealing Saddam and self-inflated moral rhetoric was not enough to seal the deal with the American people, the Bush White House also threw in an added incentive: The invasion of Iraq was not just necessary and good; it would also be a "cakewalk." Chapter five reveals how the military success of the war in Afghanistan, buttressed by the seemingly "bloodless" Gulf War I, had left Americans under the dangerous impression that they could simply bomb countries into submission, without much risk.

"The American Century foundered on the shoals of Vietnam," wrote Daniel Bell in 1975, summarizing the impact of the war on U.S. foreign policy. And so it did for two decades, until the first Gulf War revived old illusions of American power. At the time, various pundits boldly declared the end of the Vietnam Syndrome, discarded in the trash heap of history thanks to the dazzling array of the Pentagon's arsenal. But until 9/11, Americans remained unwilling to test their newfound confidence in any full-fledged, unilateral war.

If the desire for blood fueled support for the Afghan war, however, the certainty of a quick victory made such support easier to marshal the next time around. Unlike the first Gulf War, a majority (58 percent) of Americans supported invading Iraq on the eve of war—and despite reservations about the costs of going it alone. However, in neither the first Gulf War nor the overthrow of the Taliban's rule in Afghanistan had the United States committed large numbers of ground troops to actually occupying a nation.

The Bush administration lied, perhaps even to itself, about the risks of invading and occupying a nation of 24 million people. Chapter five lays bare the high price we've paid since May 1, 2003—the supposed end of this war—for the hubris of this White House which assumed that Iraqis would be content to simply play their assigned roles in its grand plan.

Finally, in chapter six, we show how these lies were supported by a nonpartisan fantasy—that at the end of the day, we would leave Iraq not only free of WMD and Saddam Hussein, but as a healthy democracy for which the Iraqis deeply would be grateful. This scenario was particularly satisfying for those who sincerely considered themselves humanitarians or internationalists; sure, there might be much suffering and death among the local people along our march to Baghdad, but in the end it would seem like small potatoes in exchange for decades or centuries of progress.

Not only was this too untrue, it didn't take into account the effect the war would have on our own democracy, as our leaders went further and further out on a limb in order to shout down the skeptics.

OF ALL THE LIES THIS administration has told its people, one false promise resonated most deeply with frightened Americans—the promise that a war with Iraq would make us safer. Instead this war has left

Americans more vulnerable than ever—our safety sacrificed at the altar of this administration's arrogance. "A-teams" of our intelligence and military apparatus were diverted to Iraq from Afghanistan and the global hunt for Al Qaeda, when it became clear we were going to war against Hussein. Having turned up no weapons of mass destruction, the United States' ponderous presence in the region has now incited a wave of new jihadis, who have poured across the broad, porous borders of Iraq at will, taking target practice at 19-year-old troops.

On September 7, 2003, Bush shocked the country in announcing he was going to be requesting $87 billion dollars to pay for military and reconstruction expenses for Iraq and Afghanistan, in addition to the $79 billion Congress had apportioned in April. This is more money than the federal government spends annually on education and roads combined, and came on the heels of revelations that the annual budget position had seesawed from a surplus under the Clinton administration to an almost $500 billion deficit under Bush in 2003.

Another $50 billion would be needed if the rest of the world didn't pitch in—which they have shown no desire to do—and this was only the beginning. On September 23, 2003, Bush made an about-face and went to the United Nations to plea for the international support he had little use for six months earlier. He remained unwilling, however, to give up any control in Iraq in exchange for cash, troops, or UN support; *compromise* is not a word in the Bush lexicon.

While the world watched Bush sourly sample some humble pie and push it away, even pro-U.S. Iraqis began to show impatience with his administration's controlling ways. The day before the UN address, the *New York Times* reported that Ahmed Chalabi, the president of the U.S.-appointed Iraqi Governing Council, had broken with his longtime White House backers and was now calling for a much faster handover of control of the country to Iraqis, as well as a moratorium on the insertion of more foreign troops.

Another brewing crisis was the handling of Iraq's economy. "Iraq was effectively put up for sale yesterday, when the U.S.-backed administration unveiled a sweeping overhaul of the economy, giving foreign companies unprecedented access to Iraqi firms which are to be sold off in a privatization windfall," reported Rory McCarthy in the *Guardian* on September 22, 2003. Many Iraqis argued that they would be unable to compete with the wealthy foreign companies, and the potential for massive resentment seems apparent.

This undermined one of the more important promises the Bush team had made about its occupation of Iraq—that it wouldn't be an excuse to loot the country. "Iraq's oil and other natural resources belong to all the Iraqi people—and the United States will respect this fact," Deputy National Security Advisor Stephen Hadley had assured the world on February 12, 2003. Yet others in the administration said before the invasion that sales from the country's oil would pay for the United States' outlay for the occupation and reconstruction—much of which was already earmarked for American-based corporations like Halliburton and Bechtel.

In the months to come, it is possible Bush will broker a face-saving deal with the United Nations, soothe or buy off our allies, and manage to put an Iraqi face on the occupation to bring more of our soldiers home. Another option, supported by some Democrats and Republicans, is to pour even more money and troops into the country, in an effort to "do this right."

If the administration ignores rising anger both at home and abroad and willfully stays its destructive course, it may well pay the price in the 2004 presidential election. Yet, whatever the next steps made by this White House, it is extremely unlikely that either Bush or the ideologues who surround him will admit any error or wrongdoing—or the high price the rest of us are paying for their failure. The Bush administration's approach is indeed bold: We are going to say and do what we want, when and where we want, and we are going to dare the world and our domestic opposition to stop us.

This book tells the story of how the American public was betrayed in its greatest hour of need. The chapters that follow will lay out exactly how a small group of men within the Bush administration led a frightened nation down a long, treacherous road from Ground Zero to a bloody, no-exit war on the streets of Baghdad.

FIRST LIE

Al Qaeda's Ties to Iraq

"We have removed an ally of Al Qaeda."
—President George W. Bush, on the deck of the USS Lincoln,
May 1, 2003

IN HIS 2003 BOOK, *Why America Slept,* journalist Gerald Posner narrates an astonishing story relayed to him by two separate government officials concerning the interrogation of Osama Bin Laden's #3 man, Abu Zubaydah, after his March 2002 capture in Pakistan by U.S. agents. Zubaydah, according to these U.S. officials in a position to know, had meticulously detailed how Al Qaeda not only received regular and massive payments funneled through high-ranking government officials in both Pakistan and Saudi Arabia, but that in the case of 9/11 these funders were told ahead of time that a huge attack against American interests was in the works, although they were not told where it would be.

Zubaydah's version of events, if true, was shocking on a moral level, but fit perfectly with what we already knew about the perpetrators of 9/11 based on government reports and news coverage. We already knew, for example, that they had numerous real-world connections to the cash and clerics of Saudi Arabia and the Islamic madrasa schools of Pakistan. And we knew that Al Qaeda training camps had long been protected by Afghanistan's Taliban, which itself had certain benefactors.

"The Taliban regime that harbored Al Qaeda in Afghanistan appears to have been largely constructed from Saudi funding by sections of Pakistan's intelligence agencies," wrote renowned British scholar John Gray, in his book *Al Qaeda and What it Means to Be Modern.*

We also knew there was no good evidence linking them to Middle Eastern countries that had previously been linked to supporting terrorism against the West, such as Libya, Syria, or Iraq.

According to Posner's sources, Zubaydah, who had been shot three times in the raid, was tortured by his captors, who turned off and on a short-acting narcotic and gave him a "truth serum" in an effort to get him to talk about past and future Al Qaeda operations. He was uncooperative, however, until he was turned over to Arab-American agents posing as Saudi security forces and held in a room designed to look like a Saudi interrogation room. The idea was that the prisoner might fear Saudi punishments so much that he might talk.

At this point, however, things took a decidedly strange turn. Rather than show fear, Zubaydah was greatly relieved to find himself in the hands of what he thought was the Saudi government, which is notoriously fond of beheading enemies of the state. Like a teen lout whose father is the police chief, he told his "Saudi" interrogators that they needed only to call a certain Saudi prince—publisher and racehorse owner Ahmed bin Salman bin Abdul Aziz—and all would be explained. Wounded and drugged, he nevertheless reeled off home and mobile phone numbers for Abdul Aziz and two other members of the Saudi royal house. (Strangely, less than four months later, all three of these Saudis—none of them over 43—would die in a span of ten days.)

"According to the now freely talking Zubaydah, he was the Al Qaeda representative in Kandahar in the summer of 1998, when [former Saudi intelligence chief] Prince Turki [Al Faisal bin Abd Al-Aziz Al-Saud], and Taliban officials, struck a deal in which Turki gave assurances that more Saudi aid would flow to the Taliban and that the Saudis would never ask for Bin Laden's extradition, so long as Al Qaeda kept its long-standing promise of directing fundamentalism away from the kingdom," wrote

Posner, who has reported for most of America's prominent news publications and written eight books.

Then, the even bigger bombshell: "Zubaydah insisted that the Saudis . . . sent money regularly to Al Qaeda" and that his royal Saudi friends had known before 9/11 that "an attack was scheduled for American soil that day. They just didn't know what it would be, nor did they want to know more than that."

Posner's revelatory book was published in late summer of 2003. Yet, this was hardly the first sign that Saudi Arabia's connections to Al Qaeda and the 9/11 attacks were deeply troubling.

As the *Washington Post* reported on August 26, 2003, "Relations between the [United States and Saudi Arabia] have been strained in recent months over allegations in a congressional report and elsewhere that wealthy Saudis have financed terror groups and that Riyadh has not moved aggressively to stem that flow of money. Intelligence experts say that funding from wealthy individuals on the Arabian Peninsula, principally Saudi Arabia, to Al Qaeda still amounts to millions of dollars a year."

Moreover, powerful Saudi clerics are infamous for exhorting followers to pursue the anti-Semitic, anti-Western interpretations of jihad similar to those that Al Qaeda is based upon. These radical interpretations of Islam have increasingly found followers among all economic classes—many of the 9/11 hijackers, 15 of 19 of whom were from Saudi Arabia, were young, middle-class men, according to the *New York Times'* Thomas Friedman, who went to Saudi Arabia to explore their roots in an effort to illuminate the question posed relentlessly after the attacks: *Why do they hate us?*

"On some estimates, per capita income in that country has fallen by around three quarters over the past twenty years. Some of this is due to falling oil prices, but much of it is a result of population growth," wrote John Gray. "Large numbers of young males face unemployment. Most of these have been schooled to view the West with deep suspicion. The combination of an expanding population and falling living standards with a fundamentalist education system renders the Saudi regime inherently unstable."

Considering all this, what is perhaps even more shocking than Zubaydah's confessions is that in Bob Woodward's bestseller, *Bush at War,* which meticulously chronicles the Bush administration's response to 9/11, the first time the nationality of the hijackers is mentioned is on page 302. In fact, the first passing reference to Saudi Arabia in the book is on page 87, and is a telling one—although Woodward seems oblivious to the irony:

"[Colin Powell] also said it would be desirable to leave somebody in the Taliban to negotiate with, and it might be possible to work with the Saudis to try to get to the Taliban, since the Saudis were the only other major government besides Pakistan that formally recognized the Taliban as the legitimate rulers of Afghanistan."

Again and again in the national security meetings, Camp David pow-wows, and internal white papers that make up most of the book, the White House's top dogs ignore this inconvenient fact and fixate on Iraq instead, without even claiming any evidence linking Hussein's regime to the attacks.

(Later, this would become more confusing, as the American public was denied access to 28 pages of Congress' definitive report on the September 11 attacks—the same pages that deal with U.S.-Saudi connections. Meanwhile, Richard Clarke, who ran the White House crisis team after the attacks, confirmed with *Vanity Fair* and others that he had OK'd an unprecedented evacuation of 150 Saudis—including relatives of Osama Bin Laden—from the United States in the hours after the destruction of the World Trade Center and the Pentagon, and while the country's passenger and commercial fleets were grounded.)

On that same page of Woodward's book, describing a NSC meeting at Camp David on September 15, 2001, Powell goes on to make a simple argument against war with Iraq in response to 9/11—they had nothing to do with it. Woodward conveyed Powell's perspective:

"Don't go with the Iraq option right away, or we'll lose the coalition we've been signing up. 'They'll view it as bait and switch—it's not what they signed up to do.' If we weren't going after Iraq before September 11, why would we be going after them now when the current outrage is not directed at Iraq, Powell asked. Nobody could look at Iraq and say it was responsible for September 11. It was important not to lose focus. 'Keep the Iraq options open if you get the linkages,' he said. 'Maybe Syria, Iran'—the chief state sponsors of terrorism in the 1980s—'but I doubt you'll get the linkages.'"

A *bait and switch*, said Powell. It was as clear an analysis of the coming war against Iraq as has been made anywhere, and it was spoken by the Secretary of State who, more than a year later, would end up being perhaps the key player in making it work.

ONE OF THE HALLMARKS of the long-running Iraq disinformation campaign led by the White House is to repeat things that aren't true until a great many people believe they are. To keep the more finicky members of the press from challenging you directly, one can employ a whole mess of outs: expressing that something "could be true," averring later that somebody "misspoke," claiming to rely on the "best intelligence" or an "educated guess." For example:

"Iraq could decide on any given day to provide a biological or chemical weapon to a terrorist group or individual terrorists," said Bush on October 7, 2002, just days before Congress was to decide whether or not to authorize the use of force against Iraq. "Alliance with terrorists could allow the Iraqi regime to attack America without leaving any fingerprints."

It is perhaps true that this *could* happen. It is also true that Pakistan, Saudi Arabia, North Korea, China, Russia, and many other countries with long-running beefs with the United States could do the same, and would probably do it better. Many things *can* happen—it is up to foreign policy leaders to figure out what is *likely* to happen and figure out the best risk-management strategies from there. Yet for Bush's team, the key agenda seemed to be to pack the words *Iraq, Saddam Hussein, Al Qaeda, terrorism,* and *9/11* together in the same sentence as often as possible.

"Some have argued that confronting the threat from Iraq could detract from the war against terror," continued Bush in Cincinnati.

> To the contrary; confronting the threat posed by Iraq is crucial to winning the war on terror ... Terror cells and outlaw regimes building weapons of mass destruction are different faces of the same evil.
>
> Some citizens wonder, after eleven years of living with this problem [of Iraq's pursuit of WMD], why do we need to confront it now? And there's a reason. We've experienced the horror of September the 11th. We have seen that those who hate America are willing to crash airplanes into buildings full of innocent people. Our enemies would be no less willing, in fact, they would be eager, to use biological or chemical, or a nuclear weapon. . . .
>
> Knowing these realities, America must not ignore the threat gathering against us. Facing clear evidence of peril, we cannot wait for the final proof—the smoking gun—that could come in the form of a mushroom cloud. . . . Understanding the threats of our time, knowing the designs and deceptions of the Iraqi regime, we have every reason to assume the worst, and we have an urgent duty to prevent the worst from occurring.

Looking at speeches like this, it becomes much easier to understand why a majority of Americans have consistently told pollsters they believe Hussein had something to do with 9/11.

And the deliberate muddying of the waters continues: In mid-September, Cheney issued the dumbfounding claim on *Meet the Press* that success in Iraq means "we will have struck a major blow right at the heart of the base, if you will, the geographic base of the terrorists who had us under assault now for many years, but most especially on 9/11."

So if the money, manpower, and shelter for Al Qaeda came from Afghanistan, Pakistan, and Saudi Arabia, then attacking Iraq was smart because it was in the same geographic area? The astounding illogic of this sentence, made by an intelligent man, was beside the point—once again Iraq and 9/11 were being mushed together in statements reaching television audiences.

A few days later, on September 17, 2003, more than two years after the attacks, Bush tersely admitted that there was no evidence linking Iraq to 9/11.

An auxiliary tactic was to drop a completely phony or irresponsible "fact" on the world—often in "off-the-cuff" remarks—and then never either defend or retract it. Some particularly gratuitous examples of this were Bush's claim on Polish television in the first weeks of the war that the U.S. had found WMD in Iraq, and his statement later that Iraq had refused to allow inspectors into the country and thus we had to invade; Dick Cheney's statement on *Meet the Press* that Iraq "had reconstituted nuclear weapons"; and National Security Advisor Condoleezza Rice's intimation that Iraq could surprise us with "a mushroom cloud."

Regardless of the immorality of such tactics, they proved astonishingly successful at influencing public opinion. Shortly before Congress voted to authorize U.S. military action against Iraq, a CBS News poll found 51 percent of Americans believed that Hussein was involved in the 9/11 attacks, and soon afterwards, the Pew Research Center reported that two-thirds of the U.S. public agreed that "Saddam Hussein helped the terrorists in the September 11 attacks."

When called on this knavery, the White House found plenty of places to wiggle. An example from a press conference with Bush's press secretary at the time, Ari Fleischer, held on September 25, 2002:

QUESTION: Yesterday in the briefing, you said that the information you have has said Al Qaeda is operating in Iraq.

Secretary of Defense Donald Rumsfeld was asked about linkages between Al Qaeda and Saddam Hussein this morning. He said very definitively that, yes, he believes there are [such linkages]. And then the president said, talking about Al Qaeda and Saddam Hussein, the danger is that they work in concert. Is the president saying that they are working in concert, that there is a relationship? Do you have evidence that supports that?

MR. FLEISCHER: No, the president is saying that's the danger. The president has repeatedly said that the worst thing that could happen is for people—the world's worst dictators with the world's worst weapons of mass destruction—to work in concert with terrorists such as Al Qaeda, who have shown an ability to attack the United States. And that's what the president has said.

QUESTION: So why—when Rumsfeld was saying, yes, there is a linkage between the two—what is he talking about?

MR. FLEISCHER: Clearly, Al Qaeda is operating inside Iraq. And the point is, in the shadowy world of terrorism, sometimes there is no precise way to have definitive information until it is too late. And we've seen that in the past. And so the risk is that Al Qaeda operating in Iraq does present a security threat, and it's cause for concern. And I think it's very understandably so.

If you're searching, Campbell, again, for the smoking gun, again I say what Secretary Rumsfeld said—the problem with smoking guns is they only smoke after they're fired.

QUESTION: I'm not looking for a smoking gun. I'm just trying to figure out how you make that conclusion, because the British, the Russians, people on the Hill that you all have briefed about all this stuff say that there isn't a linkage, that they don't believe that Al Qaeda is there working in conjunction in any way with Saddam Hussein. And there is a mountain of comments, both public and private statements that Osama Bin Laden has made about Saddam, calling him a bad Muslim, suggesting that there would be no way that the two would ever connect. So I just—if there's something, if you have some evidence that supports this, I'm just wondering why—

MR. FLEISCHER: What supports what I just said is that the president fears that the two can get together. That's what the president has said, and that's one of the reasons that he feels so strongly about the importance of fighting the war on terror.

QUESTION: So does Rumsfeld have some information that the president doesn't, that they are, in fact, working together now?

MR. FLEISCHER: Well, I'm going to take a little more detailed look at anything that you've got there. I haven't seen a verbatim quote, so I'll take a look at that.

For months and months, Fleischer and his bosses danced this dance, trying to have it both ways. In this convenient algorithm, Bush could talk ominously about the possibility of Al Qaeda and Iraq teaming up to wreak global havoc, yet didn't have to show any proof that supported this alleged combined threat.

When challenged on the scarcity of evidence to support their policies, the White House repeatedly turned the question on its head by using the "smoking gun" defense mentioned here by Fleischer. It was exceedingly dangerous, they said repeatedly, to be forced to find solid evidence that Iraq posed a real threat because we might only find this so-called smoking gun after it went off.

We can break this endlessly repeated White House stratagem down to its core elements: assert fact; when challenged, deny need for evidence; if pressed, deny the assertion; then assert it again in different words; if pressed further, demand the questioner prove statement's negative opposite, such as, "How do we know Iraq *wouldn't* give a nuclear bomb to Al Qaeda?"

In this way, Rumsfeld was able to link Iraq to Al Qaeda many, many times—sometimes implicitly, but other times explicitly. At one point he said the intelligence linking the two was "bulletproof"—when in fact, as we would find out later, the intelligence linking them had more holes than Swiss cheese.

Of course, it would be naïve to think that Hussein's security apparatus and Bin Laden's gang would never have encountered each other in the trenches of the Middle East's tortured spy vs. spy games, where double-crossers, ruthless hit men, and political puppets of all types rule the day. Here, Israel's Mossad faces Syria's Assad, a panoply of Palestinian rebel organizations compete for money and attention, and assassinations and car bombings are commonplace in several of the region's epicenters.

In this context, then, it is surprising how *little* documented contact—much less cooperation—has been alleged to have occurred between these two sworn enemies of the United States. Let's first look at what these allegations are.

In a written statement released October 7, 2002, CIA Director George Tenet argued that the CIA possessed "solid reporting of senior level contacts between Iraq and Al Qaeda going back a decade." That sounds pretty bad. Not particularly shocking, of course, since Al Qaeda has been a big player in the region since it got its start among the U.S.-sponsored, anti-Soviet mujahideen fighters of Afghanistan in the '80s. But bad.

When we look into the intelligence that supports this statement and the painfully careful way it is phrased, we get a good insight into how the Clinton-appointed Tenet was straining to deliver to his new bosses in the White House what they wanted. Basically, it was a very clumsy attempt to spin data that undermined Bush's argument for war into its exact opposite, a supporting plank of that policy.

Here's how it worked: U.S. intelligence agency records reported that tentative contacts between Saddam and Al Qaeda had taken place in the early '90s. In the years since, however, no such meetings had been uncovered, and so a continuing relationship between the two could only be speculated upon, according to CIA reports.

In other words, the intelligence showed that as far as we knew, Al Qaeda and Iraq *hadn't had meaningful contact in a decade.* To call this a relationship "going back a decade" was analogous to referring to somebody you dated a few times a decade ago as your girlfriend or boyfriend of ten years.

■　■　■

"If the only problem the United States had with Saddam Hussein's regime were its involvement with terrorism, our problems would be relatively mild. On the grand list of state sponsors of terrorism, Iraq is pretty far down—well below Iran, Syria, Pakistan, and others."

—From *The Threatening Storm: The Case for Invading Iraq* by Kenneth M. Pollack, published by the Council on Foreign Relations in 2002

ACCORDING TO THE LOGIC of those who supported the Iraq invasion, it was a no-brainer that it would make the world safer from the threat of terrorism, since the White House said Iraq was a "state sponsor" of terrorism with "links to Al Qaeda."

On the surface, this theory seemed reasonable: If a state with the resources and ruthlessness of Hussein's Iraq teamed up with a gang of zealots with the range and training of Al Qaeda, they could be a very destructive tandem. Since Hussein and Bin Laden played in the same sandbox and both despised the United States for humiliations real or perceived, would it be so strange for them to team up like a duo of super-villains seeking world domination for their own evil ends?

Well, yes, actually, it would be strange. Exceedingly so. As with many of the scary-sounding accusations Bush and his counselors threw out about Iraq, this one conveniently side-stepped any facts or analysis that would undermine a worldview in which Hussein was the New Hitler. The administration never explained what it meant that Iraq had sponsored terrorism. Against who? When? For what motive? How much? How effectively?

The reality had long been that the Iraqi dictator's forays into sponsoring or undertaking terrorist acts were constrained by a completely different set of motivations and limitations than those facing Al Qaeda. Despite its ties to Afghanistan, Al Qaeda is mobile, decentralized, and supported by a far-flung network of impassioned fundamentalists willing to die for a cause, or pay for it. Hussein's regime, in contrast, was immobile, centralized, and supported by his political and economic control of Iraq. These differences were enormously relevant when considering if Hussein really posed a serious terror threat to the United States or even Israel.

For example, consider again that Bush quote: "Alliance with terrorists could allow the Iraqi regime to attack America without leaving any fingerprints." Faced with "could" and "might" assertions like this, the press rarely if ever took a hard look at whether they even made sense, much less were based on hard evidence. For example, it would have been worthwhile in this case to ask what Hussein would stand to gain from such a strategy. If they had, many of them would have likely come to the same conclusion as Pollack, who supported preemptive war with Iraq but didn't buy the terrorism angle.

"Saddam has never given WMD to terrorists (at least to our knowledge) for the same reasons he has distanced himself from international terrorist groups in general," wrote Pollack in *The Threatening Storm: The Case for Invading Iraq.* And, "If he is uncomfortable with foreign terrorist groups because he cannot be certain how they will act and how their actions will affect his own security, this point is ten times more salient when weapons of mass destruction are involved. If Saddam were ever tied to a WMD terrorist attack, the targeted country would look to extract a fearful vengeance from him."

What the White House did know or should have known about Hussein was that his central goals were consistently the same: a) to remain in power as Iraq's dictator, and b) to look tough inside the region or in a blustery standoff with the United States as part of his constant struggle to be the leading power in his region. Hussein, while certainly a megalomaniac, is not a particularly religious man like Bin Laden, or one who seeks to impose his philosophy on the world, such as Lenin. By all expert accounts, he has long fancied himself an earthly caliph, ruling men by his wiles and the sword.

"Saddam's strategic objective appears to be to dominate the Persian Gulf, to control oil from the region, or both," wrote General Brent Scowcroft in the *Wall Street Journal* in August 2002, in an overt attempt to derail the White House's move to war with Iraq before it could gain momentum. Remember, this man was the National Security Advisor for Presidents Gerald Ford and George Bush Sr.— hardly a "Saddam-appeaser," in the memorable lexicon of conservative columnist William Safire. Scowcroft continued:

> But there is scant evidence to tie Saddam to terrorist organizations, and even less to the September 11 attacks. Indeed Saddam's goals have little in common with the terrorists who threaten us, and there is little incentive for him to make common cause with them.
>
> He is unlikely to risk his investment in weapons of mass destruction, much less his country, by handing such weapons to terrorists who would use them for their own purposes and leave Baghdad as the return address. Threatening to use these weapons for blackmail—much less their actual use—would open him and his entire regime to a devastating response by the U.S. While Saddam is thoroughly evil, he is above all a power-hungry survivor.
>
> Saddam is a familiar dictatorial aggressor, with traditional goals for his aggression. There is little evidence to indicate that the United States itself is an object of his aggression. Rather,

> Saddam's problem with the U.S. appears to be that we stand in the way of his ambitions. He seeks weapons of mass destruction not to arm terrorists, but to deter us from intervening to block his aggressive designs.

When we look at Hussein in this way—as he is, not as a cartoon reincarnation of Adolf Hitler—many of his tentative dabbles in the terror business start to make more sense. Rather than global or quixotic, they are local, pragmatic, and designed to increase his clout in his immediate neighborhood.

Having supported the Palestinian Liberation Organization before it toned down its activities a bit at Anwar Sadat's urging, for example, he later switched his support to Abu Nidal and other radical rivals to the PLO's leadership. Yet, ironically, his "support" for these groups usually meant giving them refuge in Iraq—and then restraining them from actually doing anything. It was as if Hussein wanted to look like a powerful Arab nationalist but didn't actually want them to use Iraq as a launching pad for anything that would bring down destruction upon him. To be a terrorist living in Baghdad was to be a showpiece of the dictator, kept behind glass.

This was especially true after Hussein turned westward for help in his phenomenally destructive war of attrition with Iran. Again, from Pollack:

> Saddam's increasing desperation as the Iran-Iraq War dragged on caused a major shift in his support for terrorism. As Iraq became increasingly dependent on the support of the moderate Arab states, the United States, and Europe, it began to distance itself from its former terrorist colleagues. Saad al-Bazzaz, a high-ranking Iraqi defector, claims that in the 1980s Saddam made a decision not to engage in terrorism against the West. Saddam recognized (in large part because the United States and Europe told him repeatedly) that his support for terrorism

could scuttle Western assistance with the war effort. Saddam got the message. He allowed the Abu Nidal Organization to remain in Baghdad but basically prevented it from conducting operations. Iraq became one of the most forward-leaning of the Arab governments on the issue of peace negotiations with Israel. In addition, Saddam appears to have concluded that terrorism was a dangerous game that could get him into trouble but was not of great value in accomplishing his goals.

The United States, by then a de facto ally with Iraq against fundamentalist Iran, took notice in a 1986 State Department report that "the war and Iraq's accelerated drift toward the moderate Arab camp made terrorism an even less useful—*indeed counterproductive*—weapon" [italics added]. State's take on Iraq also noted that even before this shift, its support of terrorism had been limited to the region, employed "largely to intimidate Arab moderate governments and moderate elements within the PLO."

Not surprisingly, Hussein also supported groups of varying degrees of sincerity and brutality trying to incite rebellion in neighboring Turkey and Iran. For its neighbors, these efforts at destabilization were little more than annoyances—and the kind of tit-for-tat dirty tricks that hostile neighbors engage in (think: Pakistan and India). These militias also gave Hussein another weapon to use against any Iraqis he felt were getting out of line, since they owed him their existence.

Yet for the United States, which had supported Hussein in his war against Iran, to critique such regional gamesmanship as reprehensible terrorism was to be chucking big stones from a glass house: Under the Iraqi Liberation Act, federal money—U.S. taxpayers' money—was available to fund eligible anti-Hussein factions like Ayatollah Muhammad Bakr al-Hakim's Supreme Council for the Islamic Revolution, a Shiite rebel army trained and armed by Iran that fought a vicious guerrilla war against Iraq's Ba'ath government for more than two decades. (Al-Hakim, a key postwar ally of the occupying forces, maintained that he did not receive money from the United States despite being officially eligible to do so. He was killed on August 29, 2003 in a car bomb attack in Najaf, Iraq.)

In recent years, Hussein had sought attention and Arab support by being one of the countries that provided cash to families of Palestinian suicide bombers. Over the decades, Iraq had also shown itself willing and able to directly assassinate individuals beyond its borders. Usually these were Iraqi exiles, but perhaps Hussein's boldest covert action ever was his alleged attempt to have ex-president George Bush Sr. killed on the latter's triumphant visit to Kuwait in 1993. The attempt was apparently so clumsy as to be easily "rolled up" long before Bush Sr. arrived; according to Paul Pillar's *Terrorism and U.S. Foreign Policy*, published by the Brookings Institute, U.S. intelligence officials were astonished at the inept and primitive nature of Iraq's attempts at carrying out terrorism by itself.

The neocon clique had also made strenuous, but ultimately unconvincing, attempts to link the 1993 World Trade Center attack to Hussein. According to Con Coughlin, author of *Saddam: The Secret Life:* "In an attempt to show that Ramzi Youssef, the Egyptian-born terrorist convicted of carrying out the attack, was in fact an Iraqi agent, Paul Wolfowitz, the U.S. Deputy Defense Secretary, last year sent James Woolsey, the former CIA director, with a copy of Youssef's fingerprints to Swansea University to prove that Youssef was the same person as an Iraqi student who had studied at the university. Unfortunately for Mr. Wolfowitz, the two sets of fingerprints did not match."

Despite a decade of such obsessive stalking, there is still missing in this dismal record any proof that Iraq had cooperated with radical fundamentalist terrorists in general or Al Qaeda in particular. Faced with this dearth of evidence, the White House tried to take what few lemons were lying around and make lemonade.

THE FIRST OF THESE slender tidbits was the now infamous "Prague meeting" that allegedly took place between one of the 9/11 hijackers and an Iraqi official.

This was a classic example of the Bush administration's habit of leaking a sketchy snippet grasped raw from the spy dossiers, with the eager help of sympathetic pundits and journalists who blow it completely out of proportion. Later, when the basis for the claim, exposed to the light of day, proved impossibly rickety, the proponents of war simply let it go and moved on. Here's how the technique worked in this case:

First, there was the "intriguing" bit of intelligence released with the vaguest of details into the buzzing media food chain. "Mohamed Atta, the ringleader of the hijackers, met twice with Iraqi intelligence officials in Prague during the last year," reported *Newsweek* less than six weeks after the 9/11 attacks, without citing its sources.

If true, this wouldn't have been proof that Iraq had prior knowledge of or supported the 9/11 attacks, but it certainly didn't look good. Its juicy potential was not lost on the White House hawks, who began to nurture the slender anecdote like mother hens.

Next came the pressure from the White House on U.S. intelligence agencies to burnish the item to a fine sheen. According to *New York Times* sources, "American counterterrorism specialists at the FBI and the CIA subsequently came under intense pressure to thoroughly investigate the matter."

In November of 2001, conservative *New York Times* columnist William Safire reported in his influential column that "the *undisputed fact* connecting Iraq's Saddam Hussein to the September 11 attacks is this: Mohamed Atta, who died at the controls of the airliner-missile, flew from Florida to Prague to meet on April 8 [2001] . . . with Ahmad al-Ani, the Iraqi consul" [italics added].

While the *Wall Street Journal* wrote editorials preaching about the Prague meeting as if it was the Yalta Summit for evildoers, Safire reiterated the claim and argued that there was a plot to discredit the intelligence.

"Three months ago, after the absolve-Saddam campaign began to cast doubt on the report of the Atta–al-Ani meeting at the Prague airport, Interior Minister Stanislav Gross issued a statement that '[Czech intelligence] guarantees the information, so we stick by that information,'" wrote Safire. "No backing away; on the contrary, strong reaffirmation."

By this time, however, the story was cracking a bit around the edges. Czech President Vaclav Havel had cautioned that there was only "a 70 percent" chance that the meeting had actually been observed, for example, which was sort of odd—why the uncertainty?

Next, it was the White House's turn to keep the ball in the air. A *Los Angeles Times* article in early August 2002 headlined *"U.S. Returns to Theory on Iraq September 11 Link"* quoted a senior Bush administration official as saying that "there is growing evidence" of ties between Al Qaeda and Iraq and reported that "the White House is now backing claims" that the Prague meeting in fact took place.

Of course, those White House sources were anonymous, which allowed them to defend the claim that backed their argument without being on the hook if it turned out to be baloney. The next month, however, Dick Cheney went on record, although he was clearly picking his words carefully. "[W]e have reporting . . . that places [Atta] in Prague with a senior Iraqi intelligence official a few months before the attack on the World Trade Center," he said.

When asked around the same time by CNN's Wolf Blitzer whether she could confirm the Atta–al-Ani meeting, Condoleezza Rice neatly sidestepped the question.

"We continue to look at evidence of that meeting," said Rice. "And it's just more of a picture that is emerging that there may well have been contacts between Al Qaeda and Saddam Hussein's regime. There are others. And we will be laying out the case. But I don't think that we want to try and make the case that he directed somehow the 9/11 events. That's not the issue here."

This quote was another classic of obfuscation: The evidence was still being looked at; whether or not it was true, it was part of a pattern; we will tell you more later; the details aren't important; etc. Still, Rice managed to let on that Hussein was at least not the mastermind behind Al Qaeda's attacks.

On August 12, 2002, in the first throes of the White House marketing campaign for going to war with Iraq, Fred Barnes, executive editor of the conservative *Weekly Standard,* was handed the baton. Citing Czech sources, he stated flatly that not only had "Atta, the leader of the September 11 hijackers, visited Prague twice in the fifteen months before the terrorist attacks on the World Trade Center and Pentagon, in June 2000 and April 2001, and met with an Iraqi agent at least once during the second visit," but that there were photos of the meeting.

"The story of Atta's contact with an Iraqi agent has been disputed by some American and European officials. *Time,* the *Washington Post, Newsweek,* and other publications have raised doubts about it. But last week Martin Palous, the Czech ambassador to the United States, gave me the same account of Atta's time in Prague as other Czech officials had given to [Safire]," Barnes wrote in his influential conservative magazine, going on to point out how crucial it was for Bush to convince people of the reality and importance of this linkage. "The meeting has political and international importance. A connection between Iraq and Atta, an Al Qaeda operative under Osama Bin Laden, bolsters the case for military action by the United States to remove the Saddam Hussein regime in Iraq. President Bush has repeatedly said he intends to depose Saddam—without saying when. But some European leaders and American politicians have insisted a link to September 11 is needed to justify an attack on Iraq. While the meeting might not tie Saddam directly to those attacks, it does link Iraq to the Al Qaeda terrorist network, to whom Iraqi agents might secretly have slipped biological, chemical, or nuclear weapons to be used against America."

Within the week, however, the story had been completely demolished. First, CIA Director George Tenet admitted to Congress that his agency could find no evidence to confirm that the meeting took place. Then, a front-page story in the *New York Times* left egg on the faces of

Barnes and Safire. According to reporter James Risen, the Czech Republic's President Vaclav Havel had "quietly" called the White House *earlier in the year* to debunk the story.

"Mr. Havel discreetly called Washington to tell senior Bush administration officials that an initial report from the Czech domestic intelligence agency that Mr. Atta had met with an Iraqi intelligence officer, Ahmad Khalil Ibrahim Samir al-Ani, in Prague in April 2001 could not be substantiated," said the *Times*. Apparently Havel, who had publicly supported both the 2001 Afghanistan and 2003 Iraq wars, had "moved carefully behind the scenes in the months after the reports of the Prague meeting came to light to try to determine what really happened, officials said. He asked trusted advisers to investigate, and they quietly went through back channels to talk with Czech intelligence officers to get to the bottom of the story. The intelligence officers told them there was no evidence of a meeting."

Even more damning were the details that emerged from Risen's interviews regarding just how the intelligence in question had been gathered. First of all, rather than having been reported by a professional intelligence agent immediately after the alleged meeting—as had been clearly implied by Safire and Barnes—the information had been provided by a single informant *after* the September 11 attacks had put Atta's picture on television screens the world over, and *after* the Czech press stated that records showed he had traveled to Prague.

"Officials of the [Czech] intelligence service were said to be furious that [then Prime Minister Milos] Zeman had taken the information straight to the top of the American government, before they had a chance to investigate further," reported Risen, in an echo of the anger that would soon boil over in the CIA at its own government's gross abuse of intelligence relating to Iraq.

It was apparently to save Zeman, Gross, and other Czech officials embarrassment that Havel didn't go public with the results of his investigation, but instead called the White House privately. It is useful to note that nobody at the White House seemed to feel it necessary to pass on to their media friends Safire and Barnes that the story no longer held water. Perhaps frustrated that the story would not die, Havel may have allowed the results of his investigation to find their way to the *Times*.

"Today, other Czech officials say they have no evidence that Mr. Atta was even in the country in April 2001. In fact, American records indicate he was in Virginia Beach, VA, in early April. 'The interior minister claims they did meet, but the intelligence people have told me that they didn't, that the meeting didn't happen,' a senior official said," wrote Risen. According to the *Times*, Atta had come to Prague from his home in Hamburg back in June 2000, but his stay was so short before flying out to Newark that the Czechs and Germans guessed he only went there to get cheaper airfare. If he did fly to Prague in 2001, it is quite likely he was again simply en route to Hamburg.

The Czechs even specifically debunked another angle Barnes had published, alleging that the Iraqi in question—Ahmad Khalil Ibrahim Samir al-Ani—had also been targeting, for a terrorist attack, the Radio Free Europe building in Prague's Wenceslaus Square. The only evidence for this, apparently, was that al-Ani, later kicked out of the country, had been photographed in front of the building by what the *Washington Post* later reported was a standard surveillance camera. It may well be that al-Ani was casing the joint, but it should be noted that Wenceslaus Square is the teeming commercial heart of Prague and there are plenty of other reasons to be hanging out there.

Speaking of photos, those that Barnes mentioned depicting the meeting between Atta and al-Ani have never turned up. Al-Ani himself was, though, picked up by U.S. troops in July 2003, in Iraq. One of the key backers of the White House's Iraq mission, Richard Perle, formerly of the Pentagon's Defense Policy Board, was still hopeful that this would be the big break finally proving Iraq and Al Qaeda were on intimate terms.

"If he chose to, he could confirm the meeting with Atta. It would be nice to see that laid to rest. There's a lot he could tell us," Perle told the

Washington Post. "Of course, a lot depends on who is doing the interrogating." Perle said he feared the CIA would botch it and that the agency hadn't given the story enough credence. As one might imagine, this didn't go down so well at Langley, Virginia, where CIA spokesman Bill Harlow described Perle's charge as "absurd."

"We're open to the possibility that they met, but we need to be presented with something more than Mr. Perle's suspicions," an unnamed CIA official told the *Post.* "Rather than us being predisposed, it sounds like he is. He's just shopping around for an interrogator who will cook the books to his liking."

In the end, according to Defense and intelligence sources of the *Washington Post,* the detained al-Ani denied meeting with Atta—yet the White House wouldn't let the story die. On September 14, 2003, Vice President Cheney again pressed the case for a connection between Al Qaeda and the Hussein regime on *Meet the Press,* and again he dragged out the battered Atta tale: "With respect to 9/11, of course, we've had the story . . . the Czechs alleged that Mohamed Atta, the lead attacker, met in Prague with a senior Iraqi intelligence official five months before the attack, but we've never been able to develop any more of that yet, either in terms of confirming it or discrediting it."

ON FEBRUARY 5, 2003, Secretary of State Colin Powell made his much anticipated presentation to the United Nations Security Council in a last-ditch effort to convince it of the need to back a U.S.-led invasion of Iraq. Previously, Powell had been portrayed in the media as the White House's token "dove," fighting a rearguard action against Rumsfeld and Cheney to give the world time to come around on the need to remove Hussein from power by preemptive force.

It was a crossroads moment for Powell, broadly perceived to have uncommon integrity for a politician. In fact, Powell himself believed that he had been the difference-maker in Bush's impossibly narrow 2000 election victory. In any case, the mainstream media adored him.

"Powell, we sometimes forget, is a phenomenon, a chapter from tomorrow's history books walking right in front of us," gushed *Time* at Powell's UN presentation. "It isn't just the unique resume that demands respect; it's also the presence and the personality—the unforced authenticity and effortless sense of command . . . that stills and fills a room."

No doubt, Powell has charisma and brains, and his presentation that day, replete with audio-visual aids and dramatic language, was smooth and well-reviewed. Yet within weeks, much of the complex web of intelligence bits he revealed had crumbled into dust, like a long-entombed mummy that is exposed to air. The first two-thirds were dedicated to proving Iraq's weapons posed an immediate and serious threat to the world, and we'll look at those claims in chapters to come. But in trying to rally the world to back the U.S. against Iraq, he struggled to resuscitate the flagging argument that Iraq was backing or working with Al Qaeda.

Only a few days before Powell's speech, the head of defense analysis at the International Institute for Strategic Studies in London had joined a chorus of cautious voices in questioning why the known intelligence was being stretched so far. "There would be very few people who say there is a direct link," Langton told Radio Free Europe. "I would say there is very little to suggest a direct link with Al Qaeda and the regime in Baghdad."

But Powell apparently didn't agree, or else he was being a good soldier. He did, however, by all accounts pick and choose which intelligence he was comfortable presenting—reportedly deciding, according to *U.S. News & World Report,* that some of what he had been provided by the White House or the Department of Defense was "bullshit."

He made no mention of the Prague meeting between Iraq's al-Ani and Mohamed Atta, for example, which was astonishing considering how persistently this had been pushed by the White House and sympathetic columnists. Considering the comprehensiveness of his presentation, which included numerous "facts" which U.S. intelligence agencies had little faith in, it is probably safe to assume, then, that Powell, at least, had abandoned that particular discredited piece.

Instead, Powell tried a different tack, arguing that Iraq was harboring Al Qaeda operatives. "[W]hat I want to bring to your attention today is the potentially much more sinister nexus between Iraq and the Al Qaeda terrorist network, a nexus that combines classic terrorist organizations and modern methods of murder," he said. This approach fit neatly into the Bush doctrine of preemptively attacking countries that "harbor" terrorists.

The case here rested on two claims reportedly emanating from Jordanian intelligence and Kurdish militiamen: one, that a shadowy Islamist group that controlled a piece of northern Iraq in the U.S./British-patrolled Northern No-Fly Zone was backed or controlled by Baghdad; and two, that a key Al Qaeda figure wounded in Afghanistan had received medical treatment in Baghdad and then opened a terrorist training center in that same area in the north.

The fundamentalist group's name was Ansar al-Islam, which had managed for several years to fend off attacks by the two much larger Kurdish militias that had controlled most of the north since the first Gulf War. The Al Qaeda operative in question, chemical weapons expert Abu Musab al-Zarqawi, was broadly reported to have had his leg amputated in a Baghdad hospital. Less clear, however, was whether Ansar al-Islam was anything more than a local phenomenon, what al-Zarqawi did after his treatment, and whether he had Hussein's blessings.

While Powell admitted that Ansar's few hundred militants were based in an area "outside Saddam Hussein's controlled Iraq"—the Zagros mountains abutting Iran—he argued that "Baghdad has an agent in the most senior levels of the radical organization Ansar al-Islam that controls this corner of Iraq. In 2000, this agent offered Al Qaeda safe haven in the region."

This was very unclear, especially since Powell had not claimed that Ansar al-Islam was Hussein's puppet. Was this agent of Baghdad he referred to a double-agent? When he offered Al Qaeda safe haven, was he speaking for Iraq and Hussein, or for Ansar? Or was he offering Al Qaeda safe haven throughout Iraq? Powell did not clarify.

In any case, while it was certainly true that Ansar was "radical" and probably sympathetic to Al Qaeda's anti-Western views, even the United States was officially unsure it was an actual threat: On February 24, CBS News reported that it wasn't until two weeks *after* Powell's speech that our government froze the assets of the group, and that at that time Ansar still hadn't managed to land on the formal Foreign Terrorist Organization list the United States maintains.

A bureaucratic oversight? Perhaps. But let's consider another claim made by Powell, that "the Zarqawi network helped establish another poison and explosive training center camp, and this camp is located in northeastern Iraq," in Ansar's territory.

"The network is teaching its operatives how to produce ricin and other poisons," Powell said in the dramatic oratory fashion he employed throughout the presentation. "Let me remind you how ricin works. Less than a pinch—imagine a pinch of salt—less than a pinch of ricin, eating just this amount in your food, would cause shock, followed by circulatory failure. Death comes within 72 hours and there is no antidote. There is no cure. It is fatal."

In hindsight, this seems odd. Powell, representing the most powerful nation in the history of the planet and speaking to the assembled nations of the world, was spending valuable minutes of his presentation to try to terrify the world about a poison that is no more deadly than thousands of other weapons possessed by countries all over the world. "There is no cure. It is fatal."

It is not that ricin isn't scary stuff, but the emotional pitch of Powell's argument seemed particularly glaring when looking at the sketchy facts he was presenting; one had to wonder if he wasn't overcompensating. After all, what he was actually admitting was that in an area beyond Hussein's physical control some fundamentalists may be making fairly simple poisons—and it wasn't even clear ricin was one of them.

"The network is teaching its operatives how to produce ricin and other poisons," Powell said with careful phrasing. Although many in the media reported that Powell had claimed the Ansar camp was making ricin, he actually had not said that.

All of this also begged a rather obvious question: Since this camp was in an exposed area controlled by U.S. warplanes and the place had been under surveillance for months, why couldn't they just bomb the hell out of it?

Within days of Powell's presentation, 20 foreign journalists visited the camp in question and found a dilapidated collection of shacks without indoor plumbing or the electrical capacity to produce the weapons in question. There were, reported Borzou Daragahi for the *Pittsburgh Post-Gazette,* "no obvious signs of a poison factory, nor any obvious Al Qaeda operatives. Just a group of heavily armed black-turbaned Islamists with long beards and short tempers."

According to Daragahi, a Tehran-based reporter, it was officials of the Patriotic Union of Kurdistan (PUK) who had claimed to have "culled information about chemical weapons activity from Ansar al-Islam prisoners" and "pinpointed the tiny village of Sargat as the site where the plant is located" which allegedly produced such creepy items as poison paint and cigarettes.

Upon arriving in the village and finding nothing, the PUK guys "insist[ed] that the Islamist group must have moved the evidence of chemical weapons before the journalists arrived there." Unfortunately, the PUK's statements could not be downed without some big grains of salt, since they desperately wanted the United States to invade Iraq and punish the Kurd's longtime oppressors, the Ba'athists who controlled Iraq, and Ansar itself, which "just hours after the reporters visited the Sargat site . . . shot and killed General Shawkat Haji Mushir, a prominent Kurdish minister, and several other people," according to Daragahi.

(A little background: The settlement of the first Gulf War had divided Iraq into three zones, with the north and south patrolled by

British and U.S. war planes. Between them, the PUK and their bitter rivals, the Kurdistan Democratic Party, control most of the region in a truce of convenience. The stateless Kurds are a political hot potato for all the countries in the region because of their desire for an independent homeland.)

Perhaps the most difficult-to-refute accusation Powell made about Iraq's possible ties with Al Qaeda was that a cell of the organization was working with impunity in Baghdad, with at least the tacit permission of Hussein.

"Zarqawi's activities are not confined to this small corner of northeast Iraq. He traveled to Baghdad in May of 2002 for medical treatment, staying in the capital of Iraq for two months while he recuperated to fight another day," Powell said. "During his stay, nearly two dozen extremists converged on Baghdad and established a base of operations there. These Al Qaeda affiliates based in Baghdad now coordinate the movement of people, money, and supplies into and throughout Iraq for his network, and they have now been operating freely in the capital for more than eight months."

Powell didn't say where he received this information, but it appears from his preface to the presentation that he was relying quite a bit on intelligence gleaned from Al Qaeda detainees held by the United States.

"Iraqi officials deny accusations of ties with Al Qaeda. These denials are simply not credible. Last year, an Al Qaeda associate bragged that the situation in Iraq was 'good,' that Baghdad could be transited quickly," Powell continued. This probably confused the issue more than it clarified it; Al Qaeda seemed to have little trouble "transiting" throughout the Middle East, Europe, Asia, Africa, and even the United States.

"Now let me add one other fact," concluded Powell. "We asked a friendly security service to approach Baghdad about extraditing Zarqawi and providing information about him and his close associates. This service contacted Iraqi officials twice and we passed details that should have made it easy to find Zarqawi. The network remains in Baghdad. Zarqawi still remains at large, to come and go." If all this were true, it would be pretty damning stuff. Yet, here too, we find vagueness in key language that makes it seem as if Powell was hedging: ". . . we passed details that should have made it easy to find Zarqawi."

It is certainly plausible that if Hussein wasn't aiding Zarqawi, he was at least not eager to bust him for the United States. The possibility that the two might have been following a live-and-let-live relationship was hinted at by Powell himself.

"Going back to the early- and mid-1990s when Bin Laden was based in Sudan, an Al Qaeda source tells us that Saddam and Bin Laden reached an understanding that Al Qaeda would no longer support activities against Baghdad." Translation: Saddam and Bin Laden cut a deal whereby they would agree not to try to kill each other. This hardly sounded like the bonds of blood brothers—more like pragmatism on the part of two ruthless thugs with plenty of other archenemies to worry about.

Thus, if we are properly following Powell's case for war on Iraq as laid out in his Security Council speech, it amounted to this: If you are not an enemy of our enemy, you are an enemy to us. Not only did this have a certain internal logic, it was actually an expression in Powell's more refined tones of the apocalyptic sentiments Bush had been shouting since 9/11: *You're either with us or against us.*

SECOND LIE

Iraq's Chemical and Biological Weapons

"We have seen intelligence over many months that they have chemical and biological weapons, and that they have dispersed them and that they're weaponized and that, in one case at least, the command and control arrangements have been established."

—Defense Secretary Donald Rumsfeld, March 24, 2003, *Face the Nation*

"For those who say we haven't found the banned manufacturing devices or banned weapons, they're wrong, we found them."

—President Bush, June 1, 2003

". . . the American leading the hunt for banned weapons in Iraq says his team has not found any of the unconventional weapons cited by the Bush administration as a principal reason for going to war, federal officials with knowledge of the findings said today."

—Douglas Jehl and Judith Miller, writing in the *New York Times*, September 24, 2003

AS THE DOG DAYS of August 2003 dragged on, with relentlessly bad news coming out of Iraq highlighted by a series of massive, deadly, and successful bombings, a very strange story landed in the *Los Angeles Times*. "*U.S. Suspects It Received False Iraq Arms Tips*," read the headline. "Intelligence officials are reexamining data used in justifying the war. They say Hussein's regime may have sent bogus defectors."

The story, based primarily on interviews with unnamed senior U.S.

intelligence officials, was another embarrassing episode for the White House and the CIA. "Frustrated at the failure to find Saddam Hussein's suspected stockpiles of chemical and biological weapons, U.S. and allied intelligence agencies have launched a major effort to determine if they were victims of bogus Iraq defectors who planted disinformation to mislead the West before the war."

This was one for the truth-is-stranger-than-fiction files. Hussein was trying to make himself look more rogue than he really was?

"Baghdad apparently tricked legitimate defectors into funneling phony tips about weapons production and storage sites," stated *Times* staff writer Bob Drogin. Said one of his sources: "They were shown bits of information and led to believe there was an active weapons program, only to be turned loose to make their way to Western intelligence sources. Then, because they believe it, they pass polygraph tests . . . and the planted information becomes true to the West, even if it was all made up to deceive us."

Actually, if true, the bizarre report would go a long way toward explaining one of the great mysteries of Hussein's Iraq in light of the complete absence of WMD discoveries after the war: Why, if he wasn't violating the UN sanctions on his weapons programs, did he always act so damn guilty? After all, Hussein's state-controlled press had thundered of the great "progress" of the country's scientific "nuclear mujahideen," even as it was under mandates not to pursue nuclear weapons design or production. Why give the United States an excuse for regime change?

The question was not an academic one, or something for pop psychologists to debate on websites devoted to dictators and mass murderers, because Hussein's goals and actions were the ostensible core reason for the invasion. Many a White House or Pentagon official had played Hussein's counter-intuitive behavior as a supposed trump card, and when Rumsfeld was challenged after the invasion about the missing WMD, he seemed to care not at all if they turned up or were simply another one of Hussein's bluffs.

So could Saddam really have been so stupid as to trick the United States into deposing him? The answer is yes. Despite his long and terrible reign, he has made major miscalculations in the past—most notably in underestimating the West's will to enter the fray in the Middle East.

In 1990, he famously—and impulsively—believed he could take Kuwait without intervention, for example, reportedly telling his generals at the last moment to keep rolling forward on what they had thought was a limited action to seize oil fields on Iraq's border with the emirate. Yet, he was rolled back by the broadest military coalition formed in decades, faced armed revolts in the north and south, and was lucky to have stayed in power under greatly reduced circumstances.

It is also hard to believe, in hindsight, that he was so reckless as to think it wise to try to assassinate President George Bush Sr. in 1993, as he is purported to have done; had he been successful, 90 percent of Americans would have been demanding his head on a stick by nightfall.

While he couldn't read the West so well, he was undeniably an astonishingly shrewd player at home and in the region. And, right or wrong, it was here where his deepest fear (being overthrown by his own regime) and wildest fantasy (becoming a caliph ruling the whole Arab world) likely were seated. And in Iraq and throughout the Arab world, he believed, it was perceived power and public bravery in the face of the powerful West that were the true coins of the realm.

Thus, while Rumsfeld, et al., either couldn't see it or didn't want to, there was a very plausible rationale for all of Hussein's contradictory, obstructionist, confrontational, and flatly irritating behavior between his two wars with the United States. He continually played chicken with the United States, played cat-and-mouse with UN weapons inspectors, and played himself as a bombastic modern Nebuchadnezzar for the Arab world. Like a troubled bully, he couldn't live without the United States' hostile attention or the ability to strike fear in his neighbors.

So would it make sense for him to exaggerate his military capabilities? Of course. Hussein's goal was to be menacing, which is a matter of appearances as much as reality. In no way is this to deny that he *wanted* to have every horrific weapon that the United States had ever possessed, whether nuclear, biological, chemical, or conventional. But, if he was prevented from having them, you can bet he was going to be damn sure not to let on his weaknesses to his many enemies. This is simply the logic of the wounded animal.

The *Los Angeles Times'* Drogin and his sources put it similarly: "Hussein's motives for such a deliberate disinformation scheme may have been to bluff his enemies abroad, from Washington to Tehran, by sending false signals of his military might. Experts also say the dictator's defiance of the West, and its fear of his purported weapons of mass destruction, boosted his prestige at home and was a critical part of his power base in the Arab world."

In fact, Powell also said his arguments were based partly on information provided by Iraqi defectors. And one can easily imagine other, much simpler ways to accomplish the same effect. Consider that in Colin Powell's long, detailed presentation to the United Nations Security Council on February 5, 2003, one of his linchpin pieces of intelligence was intercepted radio communications in which Iraq's military officers appeared to be making references to WMD. It wouldn't be hard to script such conversations with the idea of being conveniently overheard.

Of course, intelligence of dubious provenance is the norm in the spy game. That's why at the core of any working intelligence agency are hoards of analysts who scrutinize the reams of information being generated through human and electronic means. It's a difficult job, and highly sensitive to either poor practices or political pressure. Most dangerous of all is to make the data fit your beliefs, rather than vice versa. Yet that was exactly what happened.

"We were prisoners of our own beliefs," a senior U.S. weapons expert who had just recently returned from a stint with the United States' Iraq Survey Group, the 1,400-member team responsible for the search for illicit weapons, told the *Los Angeles Times* in Drogin's story. "We said

Saddam Hussein was a master of denial and deception. Then, when we couldn't find anything, we said that proved it, instead of questioning our own assumptions."

Of course, there is one other possibility, a frightening one: that Hussein's loyalists managed to disperse biological and chemical weapons to terrorists or keep them for a guerrilla war after their inevitable defeat against the U.S. military juggernaut. As of early September 2003, however, no such weapons had been used in attacks and nobody had publicly reported if or how they may have been dispersed.

On April 21, 2003, *New York Times* reporter Judith Miller made a bizarre report from wartime Iraq that pressed this thesis. According to Miller's U.S. military commander sources, they had found a scientist who claimed that Iraq had destroyed its chemical weapons only days before the war, had sent WMD materiel to Syria, and had ties to Al Qaeda. Miller was not allowed to meet this man, whom she could see in the distance wearing a baseball cap.

However, this story, like numerous other "finds" reported breathlessly on Fox News during the first heady weeks of the war, faded away without any echo. And, as Seth Ackerman wrote for the nonprofit media watchdog organization, Fairness & Accuracy In Reporting (FAIR), Miller was "within the press, perhaps the most energetic disseminator of 'inactionable intelligence' on Iraq's putative weapons ... A veteran of the Iraqi WMD beat, Miller has accumulated a bulging clippings file over the years full of splashy, yet often maddeningly unverifiable, exposés alleging various Iraqi arms shenanigans: 'Secret Arsenal: The Hunt for Germs of War' (2/26/98); 'Defector Describes Iraq's Atom Bomb Push' (8/15/98); 'Iraqi Tells of Renovations at Sites For Chemical and Nuclear Arms' (12/20/01); 'Defectors Bolster U.S. Case Against Iraq, Officials Say' (1/24/03)."

If the headlines of Judith Miller's stories sounded like they were written by Donald Rumsfeld, Richard Perle, and the whole gang at the Project for the New American Century, there was a good reason—they shared the same intelligence source: Ahmed Chalabi and the Iraqi National Congress. Both Rumsfeld's shadow intelligence agency, OSP, and PNAC were heavily reliant on Chalabi and the INC's motley collection of defectors and exiles for their understanding of Iraq, and so was Miller, as she admitted in an email to a colleague made public by the *Washington Post*'s media critic, Howard Kurtz.

"I've been covering Chalabi for about 10 years," Miller wrote. "He has provided most of the front-page exclusives on WMD to our paper."

Chalabi was a political animal with a clear agenda—entreat, prod, or manipulate the United States to overthrow Saddam Hussein and facilitate his own rise to power—and for a Pulitzer Prize–winning journalist to fall for it is disturbing. As Seth Ackerman said, citing a United Press International report on Chalabi in March 2003, "He was known in Washington foreign-policy circles as a primary source for many of the weapons allegations that career CIA analysts greeted with skepticism, but that Pentagon hawks promoted eagerly." Couldn't Miller have exerted some skepticism as well?

In any case, by 2003, Chalabi was becoming a modest household name in the United States, the Beltway's favorite Iraqi who was not-so-subtly tabbed by the White House as the man to lead a post–regime change Iraq. Unfortunately, however, Chalabi had not himself been in Iraq since 1958, and by the looks of it in hindsight, the WMD intelligence he and his comrades in the Iraqi National Congress passed onto Rumsfeld and Miller might have been nearly as stale.

According to a *New York Times* article published September 28, 2003:

> An internal assessment by the Defense Intelligence Agency has concluded that most of the information provided by Iraqi defectors who were made available by the Iraqi National Congress was of little or no value, according to federal officials briefed on the arrangement.
>
> In addition, several Iraqi defectors introduced to American

intelligence agents by the exile organization and its leader, Ahmed Chalabi, invented or exaggerated their credentials as people with direct knowledge of the Iraqi government and its suspected unconventional weapons program, the officials said.

The arrangement, paid for with taxpayer funds supplied to the exile group under the Iraq Liberation Act of 1998, involved extensive debriefing of at least half a dozen defectors by defense intelligence agents . . . the officials said. But a review early this year by the Defense Agency concluded that no more than one-third of the information was potentially useful, and efforts to explore those leads since have generally failed to pan out, the officials said.

Before the war, though, Iraq was described by the White House as brimming with biological and chemical weapons of all types and descriptions.

"Our conservative estimate is that Iraq today has a stockpile of between 100 and 500 tons of chemical weapons agent. That is enough to fill 16,000 battlefield rockets," Powell told the United Nations Security Council a few weeks before the war. He pointed to satellite photos that allegedly showed activity indicative of development, movement, and storage of biological and/or chemical weapons.

"We know where [Iraq's WMD] are," Defense Secretary Rumsfeld assured reporters on March 30, 2003. "They're in the area around Tikrit and Baghdad and east, west, south, and north somewhat."

This latter statement was confusing in more ways than one. If Rumsfeld knew so clearly where the illicit weapons were located, why hadn't he bothered to share this information with UN weapons inspectors on the ground in Iraq, before chasing them out of the country when he launched the war?

In fact, the chiefs of both UN and IAEA teams of inspectors had already gone public by this point with their extreme frustration at the

United States' resistance to share the intelligence that would back up its claims about Iraqi WMD.

The relationship between the White House and the inspectors had reached its nadir, with the Bush administration leaders saying that the inspectors wouldn't find anything no matter how hard they looked, and picking mercilessly at every failure, real or perceived, in the on-again, off-again inspection regime of a dozen years. Foremost among these "hall of shame" examples trotted out regularly was the story of Hussein Kamel.

Kamel, Saddam Hussein's son-in-law, had defected back in 1995 from Iraq and revealed that he had himself directed an Iraqi WMD program that before the 1991 Gulf War had been more advanced than anybody had known. In the following weeks, Iraqi officials took inspectors to Kamel's farm, revealing hundreds of thousands of pages of documents that detailed Iraq's secret successes in weaponizing biological agents, building ballistic missiles, and producing chemical weapons.

With typical disregard for how ridiculous it sounded, Iraqi officials claimed Kamel was pursuing the weapons on his own initiative. Strangely, a few months later in 1996, Kamel decided to slip back into the country—where he was quickly and unsurprisingly killed.

Those who wanted the United States to have a more aggressive Iraq policy held up the Kamel story not as a victory for a patient policy of containment and inspection, but as another example of Hussein's endless capability for mischief and the cluelessness of the inspectors. Furthermore, since Kamel was briefed in secret seven years earlier and was now dead, it was quite easy to twist his words to various uses.

"In 1995, after several years of deceit by the Iraqi regime, the head of Iraq's military industries defected," said Bush in his October 7, 2002 speech. "It was then that the regime was forced to admit that it had produced more than 30,000 liters of anthrax and other deadly biological agents. The inspectors, however, concluded that Iraq had likely produced two to four times that amount. This is a massive stockpile of biological weapons that has never been accounted for, and capable of killing millions."

"It took years for Iraq to finally admit that it had produced four tons of the deadly nerve agent, VX," Powell told the UN Security Council several months later. "A single drop of VX on the skin will kill in minutes. Four tons. The admission only came out after inspectors collected documentation as a result of the defection of Hussein Kamel, Saddam Hussein's late son-in-law."

What Powell and Bush failed to note was that Kamel had *also* said that "after the Gulf War [of 1991], Iraq destroyed all its chemical and biological weapons stocks and the missiles to deliver them." In other words, according to the same source, these huge stockpiles that Kamel told us about and our president used to scare us with, didn't actually exist any longer and hadn't for about a decade.

According to a *Newsweek* article printed a few weeks before the war began, the CIA and Britain's intelligence agency had heard Kamel's story eight years earlier, and "a military aide who defected with Kamel [also] backed Kamel's assertions about the destruction of WMD stocks."

Furthermore, according to an article by Seth Ackerman in Fairness & Accuracy In Reporting's July/August edition of *Extra!* that cited a 1999 UN report, "Using forensic techniques, the inspectors confirmed that Iraq indeed 'undertook extensive, unilateral, and secret destruction of large quantities of proscribed weapons.'"

This was a bombshell exploding, but few heard it go off; it was an old and complicated story, and by now, with the war days away, most of America had already chosen sides and was hunkered down to see what would happen. It didn't help that *Newsweek* played down the story, running it in its "Periscope" section of short pieces instead of as a major feature story, nor that Kamel was, because of his past, a suspicious character.

Yet, it did manage to elicit an angry response from CIA spokesperson Bill Harlow. "It is incorrect, bogus, wrong, untrue," he told Reuters on February 24, 2003. But two days later, according to FAIR's Ackerman, a complete copy of the Kamel transcript—drawn from an internal UN inspectors' document stamped "sensitive"—was obtained by Glen

Rangwala of Cambridge University and posted on the Internet. After that, the administration didn't say much about Hussein Kamel.

According to Kamel's statement as presented by the UN document, Iraq destroyed its actual WMD but kept its plans for how to build them intact in hidden blueprints, computer disks, microfiches, and production molds, so that they could be recreated in the event the inspectors left the country. While this showed once again in what bad faith all of Hussein's promises were offered, it also was a clear argument for the effectiveness of inspections as a deterrent to his WMD efforts.

The history of weapons inspections is rather tortuous, marred by UN and U.S. politicization of its goals and means, as well as Iraq's tenacity in never giving an inch more than was demanded. The CIA abused the process by infiltrating the inspector teams, while Baghdad's balkiness forced those managing the process to regularly threaten force to make it comply. Nevertheless, it is generally agreed that by 1996 the inspectors had fundamentally destroyed the equipment and facilities that would be needed to build new WMD.

"We felt that in all areas we have eliminated Iraq's [WMD] capabilities fundamentally," said former chief inspector Rolf Ekeus, in May 2000 at Harvard.

What was less clear—if you didn't believe Kamel, or, like Bush, only believed him where it was convenient—was what had happened to Iraq's pre–Gulf War stocks of weaponized chemical and biological agents. There was a big discrepancy between what Iraq's inventories said it once had and what the inspectors had been able to document and/or destroy. The gap— "26,000 liters of anthrax, 38,000 liters of botulin, one-and-a-half tons of nerve agent VX, and 6,500 aerial chemical bombs" sitting ready to use "in 45 minutes"—became almost a mantra of the Bush administration, repeated by Powell, Fleischer, and others at every opportunity.

Never mind that if these stocks existed, they would be hopelessly degraded and in many cases impotent. Nerve agents sarin and tabun have a shelf life of five years, VX a bit longer; botulinum toxin and liquid anthrax, if kept in ideal conditions, are potent for about three years. Mustard gas is perhaps the most stable of the agents Iraq had possessed, yet according to former UN weapons inspector Scott Ritter, by 2003 any remaining biological or chemical weapons stores there were now at least a dozen years old and had reverted to "harmless, useless goo."

(Some in the media have portrayed Ritter, a tough-guy U.S. marine, as a crank—apparently because he "switched sides" and became an outspoken critic of the Bush propaganda campaign on Iraq. In fact, a close reading of his books shows Ritter's position had not flipped, but rather had evolved. In *Endgame,* for example, his basic analysis was that the United States and UN should commit to *either* an earnest and consistent policy of nonproliferation containment or invade, knock down the government, and usher in a new and better one.)

Even more skeptical about the current state of Iraq's chemical weapons was the Pentagon itself, as journalist Cliff Montgomery reported on AlterNet on May 8, 2003. According to the Department of Defense's "Militarily Critical Technologies List" (MCTL) written in 1998 and updated in 2002, Iraq produced nerve gases that were poorly produced and "inherently unstable."

"They had to get the agent to the front promptly or have it degrade in the munition," the DOD report continued, noting that the shelf life for such agents was only a matter of weeks. "The chemical munitions found in Iraq after the [first] Gulf War contained badly deteriorated agents and a significant proportion were visibly leaking."

Now, remember, this is *before* the first Gulf War, when by all accounts Iraq's military machine was at its apex. Yet the DOD report dryly noted how primitive some of Iraq's WMD efforts were even then: "The Iraqis had a small number of bastardized binary munitions in which some unfortunate individual was to pour one ingredient into the other from a jerry can prior to use." (Binary munitions are ones where two substances that react to make a poison or explosive are kept separate until the weapon is actually used.)

So, let's review: We have a whole mess of White House allegations about a huge stockpile of chemical and biological weapons that very possibly had been destroyed a decade earlier and, if not, was likely quite degraded and difficult to deliver to a target.

Is this too harsh? Not when we consider that after the U.S. took control of Iraq and toppled Hussein, Kamel's version, and Ritter's, looked much more accurate than Bush's. For one thing, despite an astonishing string of false alarms trumpeted by the electronic media in the first heady days of the invasion, not a single vial of chemical or biological weapons has been found in occupied Iraq. And secondly, despite being freed from Hussein's tyranny, the country's weapons scientists insisted that the country's chemical and biological weapons stores had been destroyed years earlier, although it appeared likely the recipes had been kept somewhere.

According to Ackerman's review of the press, "With remarkable unanimity, former Iraqi scientists interviewed since the war about the status of the weapons programs—including VX specialist Emad Ani, presidential science advisor Lieutenant General Amer al-Saadi, nuclear scientist Jafar Jafar, and chief UN liaison Brigadier General Ala Saeed—have all maintained that the regime did, in fact, destroy these stockpiles in the early 1990s, as it claimed. According to a U.S. intelligence official, the top scientists are all 'sticking to the party line, that Saddam destroyed all his WMD long ago,' the *Los Angeles Times* reported [on April 27, 2003]."

Asked about stories like these by journalists wondering why we hadn't known this before, Bush complained that he was being abused by "revisionist historians."

THE PROBLEM WITH exaggeration, of course, is if you get found out, your credibility is shot—rather like the little boy who cried wolf. In the summer of 2003, under pressure over phony claims that Iraq had tried to buy enriched uranium from Africa, the White House took the highly unusual step of abruptly releasing part of a key classified document that was the U.S. intelligence community's most authoritative assessment of the Iraqi threat.

It was this document, known as the National Intelligence Estimate (NIE) and selectively distributed within the government in October 2002, that had been so crucial to Bush in stoking the Iraqi WMD mythos through the winter. And once again the strategy ultimately backfired, because the classified intelligence, exposed to scrutiny, proved so weak.

(It is interesting to note that before the Senate voted overwhelmingly to authorize the use of force in Iraq, only the members of that body's Select Intelligence Committee got to see the classified version of the NIE—and they voted 5–4 against authorization. Much later, in September 2003, a bipartisan Congressional committee reviewing the material used to compile the NIE would deem the data outdated, circumstantial, and fragmentary—and wholly insufficient to come to the conclusion that Iraq possessed chemical and biological weapons and had links to Al Qaeda.)

The first paragraph of the NIE summary starts out with a tone of total authority . . . except for the final and parenthetical sentence: "We judge that Iraq has continued its weapons of mass destruction (WMD) programs in defiance of UN resolutions and restrictions. Baghdad has chemical and biological weapons as well as missiles with ranges in excess of UN restrictions; if left unchecked, it probably will have a nuclear weapon during this decade. (See INR alternative view at the end of these Key Judgments)."

(The "alternative view" by the State Department's intelligence branch was in a clearly labeled and quite readable box of text. Later, the White House would refer to this as a "footnote" that hadn't caught Rice or Bush's eyes.)

Reading on between the many bold assertions, we learn that "we lack specific information on many key aspects of Iraq's WMD programs," and that many of the judgments are speculations based on valid, yet circumstantial evidence, such as Iraq's past patterns of behavior, the fact that it had some new oil money to throw around, and that UN inspectors had been out of the country for several years.

Also strange, especially upon a second or third reading, is that even in the NIE, there is a palpable sense of exaggerated threat. For example, it remarks on the first page of the summary that "Baghdad has exceeded UN range limits of 150 km with its ballistic missiles and is working with unmanned aerial vehicles (UAVs), which allow for a more lethal means to deliver biological and, less likely, chemical warfare agents." Bush emphasized both these claims in his fall speeches, where they sounded quite scary. Shine a little light on them, however, and both seem considerably less threatening.

The missiles in question, al-Samoud and Ababil-100, are short-range weapons which were deemed by some analysts—and not others—to be in marginal violation of the range limits, reaching "perhaps as far as 300 km," says the NIE. These were the missiles being dismantled when UN inspectors were shooed out of the country by Bush's announcement of imminent war in mid-March 2003.

For their part, the talk about so-called UAVs—a complicated way to say "drones"—was straightforward. The NIE claimed, "Baghdad's UAVs could threaten Iraq's neighbors, U.S. forces in the Persian Gulf, *and if brought close to, or into, the United States, the U.S. Homeland*" [italics in the original]. Yet this is preposterous because of the primitive nature of Iraq's UAV prototypes and program; and a red herring, because if Iraq wanted to and could smuggle WMD into the United States, why would it need a UAV to disperse it? It could just be dropped at the nearest mall, or out of a crop duster. But hey, "unmanned aerial vehicles" certainly sounds scary, doesn't it?

As it happened, the Air Force was also skeptical of The Great Iraqi UAV Threat and expressed this in the NIE: "The Director, Intelligence, Surveillance, and Reconnaissance, U.S. Air Force, does not agree that Iraq is developing UAVs *primarily* intended to be delivery platforms for chemical and biological warfare (CBW) agents. The small size of Iraq's new UAV strongly suggests a primary role of reconnaissance, although CBW delivery is an inherent capability" [italics in the original].

(On September 26, 2003, the *Washington Post* interviewed the Air Force's senior intelligence expert, who said nothing he had seen since the occupation had changed his office's estimates on the capabilities of Iraq's UAVs. The tiny planes found by U.S. troops simply had no room to carry chemical or biological weapons, Robert S. Boyd told the *Post*. "Why would you purposefully design a vehicle to be an inefficient delivery means? Wouldn't it make more sense that they were purposefully designing it to be a decent reconnaissance UAV?" Boyd also specifically rebutted a scary statement made by Powell in his UN Security Council address describing an elaborate effort to develop "spray devices that could be adapted for UAVs" as bogus, noting that the devices were too heavy for the drones Iraq was building.)

Much of the rest of the "Key Judgments" of the NIE were dedicated to guessing how and under what circumstances Hussein would use his WMD in a war with the United States. "He probably would use CBW [chemical/biological weapons] when he perceived he irretrievably had lost control of the military and security situation," the document speculated, also guessing that "Iraq probably would attempt clandestine attacks against the U.S. Homeland if Baghdad feared an attack that threatened the survival of the regime were imminent or unavoidable, or possibly for revenge." Another bullet point wondered if "Saddam, if sufficiently desperate, might decide that only an organization such as Al Qaeda . . . could perpetuate the type of terrorist attack that he would hope to conduct."

Whether because he didn't have such weapons, or decided not to use them, none of these scenarios came to pass.

Once the inspectors were on the ground, things got rather surreal, because the more Iraq caved under the pressure of the UN inspectors and surrounding gauntlet of troops, the more dismissive the United States became of the possibility that war could be avoided. The White

House's public line had hardened—at this point it wouldn't matter if Iraq turned its swords into ploughshares, and so the world watched the odd sight of a nation being disarmed just as it was about to be invaded.

In fact, it appeared that Hussein was one of the last to grasp that the United States really didn't care what he did or didn't possess. Somebody was going to pay for 9/11 and he had been selected, for his visibility, ugliness, vulnerability, and oil resources.

But the durable tyrant was now backpedaling, fast. The Iraqis gave in to each new demand made by the inspectors, who already had the run of the country. Consequently, the inspectors were able to verify Iraq's destruction of 50 of 75 missiles in violation of parameters on range; held private meetings with Iraqi weapons scientists; visited locations where biological and chemical weapons were destroyed in 1991; and gained permission for U2 spy plane flyovers.

It was suggested by some pundits that if this renewed spirit of acquiescence were to continue apace, the United States and Britain would be wise to simply declare victory and go home, Hussein and his fundamentally unstable nation once again successfully contained, perhaps even neutered. And if some of the administration's statements were to be believed, it was still possible to avoid war.

On January 30, 2003, Bush said, "I will tell my friend Silvio [Berlusconi, prime minister of Italy] that the use of military troops is my last choice, not my first." The next week, Rumsfeld, visiting Munich, claimed, "We still hope that force may not be necessary to disarm Saddam Hussein. . . . Let me be clear: No one wants war."

A week later, however, Henry Kissinger—who had been appointed by Bush as head of the 9/11 investigation but then was forced to resign over conflicts of interest—echoed the conventional wisdom prevailing in Beltway and media circles. "If the United States marches 200,000 troops into the region and then marches them back out," Kissinger said in the *Washington Post* on February 10, "the credibility of American power . . . will be gravely, perhaps irreparably impaired."

Nobody watching the White House believed Hussein could do anything now to prevent the invasion. The reality was, though, that his fate had already been sealed for months. Iraq's stepped-up cooperation with the UN was simply another distraction from the White House's predetermined goal, formalized internally the previous August.

For many moderate career diplomats and intelligence analysts who prided themselves on their common sense realism, however, this was all going way too far. It was one thing to bluff a bluffer like Hussein, but to subordinate foreign policy to a risky land war and occupation in the Mideast? And to base this all on weak intelligence and the think-tank fantasies of a bunch of trigger-happy neoconservatives? They could see the train wasn't going to stop at a station and, in fact, was liable to run off a cliff.

The result was the historic emergence of a series of whistle-blowers from inside the system who threw away secure careers to give the lie to what their government was doing.

"We have not seen such systematic distortion of intelligence, such systematic manipulation of the American people, since the war in Vietnam," wrote John Brady Kiesling, a 20-year veteran of the U.S. Foreign Service in his letter of resignation February 27, 2003 to Secretary of State Powell. Kiesling, who was a political counselor in U.S. embassies throughout the Mideast, added that "until this administration, it had been possible to believe that by upholding the policies of my president, I was also upholding the interests of the American people and the world. I believe it no longer."

Later came Gregory Thielmann, who had served as a director in the State Department's Bureau of Intelligence until his retirement in September and had access to the classified reports that formed the basis for the U.S. case against Saddam spelled out by President Bush and his aides. Thielmann noted that U.S. intelligence on Iraq was spotty and inconsistent, but emphasized that the real problem "lies with the way senior officials misused the information they were provided.

"Iraq posed no imminent threat to either its neighbors or to the United States," Thielmann added.

For his part, Bush responded to these accusations with an accusation of his own, claiming his critics were "trying to rewrite history." Rumsfeld told the Senate that war with Iraq had become inevitable not because of fresh evidence of weapons of mass destruction but because Washington saw what evidence there was prior to 2001 "in a dramatic new light" after September 11.

Paul Wolfowitz, one of the generals' top civilian bosses in the Pentagon and a key proponent of invading Iraq, certainly seemed unconcerned with the implications of making arguments for war based on convenience rather than facts. In a *Vanity Fair* interview, he said, "The truth is that for reasons that have a lot to do with the U.S. government bureaucracy, we settled on the one issue that everyone could agree on, which was weapons of mass destruction, as the core reason."

Wolfowitz did list two other reasons: to fight terrorism and Hussein's criminal treatment of the Iraqi people. However, Wolfowitz dismissed the last reason, saying, "the third one, by itself . . . is a reason to help the Iraqis but it is not a reason to put American kids' lives at risk, certainly not on the scale [that] we did it." Yet in many, many White House comments and speeches, this last argument—the one behind the name given to the invasion, Operation Iraqi Freedom—would move to the forefront as the others were knocked down one by one.

Problem was, the palpable anger of betrayal felt by men like Kiesling and Thielmann was being backed up on the ground with facts. While London and Washington continued to promise, almost forlornly, that WMD would still be found in Iraq—and if not actual weapons, then "programs" or "a paper trail"—the Marines who controlled the ground in Iraq were baffled at how clean the place was turning out to be. When Lieutenant General James Conway, commander of the 1st Marine Expeditionary Force, was asked at the end of May 2003 why his Marines failed to encounter or uncover any of the weapons of mass destruction that U.S. intelligence had warned them about, his straightforwardness was refreshing.

"We were simply wrong," Conway said. "It was a surprise to me then, it remains a surprise to me now, that we have not uncovered [nuclear, chemical, or biological] weapons, as you say, in some of the forward dispersal sites." He added, "Believe me, it's not for lack of trying. We've been to virtually every ammunition supply point between the Kuwait border and Baghdad, but they're simply not there."

"What the regime was intending to do in terms of its use of the weapons, we thought we understood or we certainly had our best guess, our most dangerous [scenario], our most likely courses of action that the intelligence folks were giving us," Conway told Pentagon reporters. "We were simply wrong."

Now that the "imminent threat" posed by Iraqi chemical or biological weapons had turned out not to be so imminent, the question was: Did our spy operations blow the call, or was the dope they developed distorted or exaggerated by our political leaders? Thielmann, Kiesling, and skeptics like Paul Krugman of the *New York Times* had weighed in against the White House, but the story had not yet caught fire. The media and the Democrats were still too nervous to question the purpose of our being in Iraq, lest they be shamed for "not supporting our troops."

In London, however, British Prime Minister Tony Blair was feeling real political heat for arguing so strenuously before the invasion that Hussein posed an immediate threat—and using such questionable facts as the claim that before the allied invasion, Saddam Hussein had "existing and active military plans for the use of chemical and biological weapons, which could be activated within 45 minutes." This terrifying-sounding claim was pure hogwash: If you had battlefield weapons, wouldn't you expect them to be ready to use within 45 minutes? The claim was also later shown to be based on a single Iraqi source who, British intelligence sources said, probably wouldn't have had access to such information.

Blair's problems were exponentially compounded when scientist David Kelly, believed to have leaked a critique of Britain's own version of the NIE to the BBC, was found dead, an apparent suicide, after being outed by the government as a whistle-blower. As a sad footnote, one of his colleagues told a British newspaper that he and Kelly had laughed over how the "45 minutes" claim had been so wrongly interpreted, since they believed the source in question had meant that it would take that long for Hussein simply to contact his WMD commanders in the event of a war situation.

(These revelations, however, were too late to save Bush further embarrassment: He used the 45 minutes claim, without citing the British as the source, in a national radio address—proving once again that the same few bits of shaky intelligence were getting systematically recycled by the war propaganda machine.)

With the allies not finding any WMD, whether deployed or not, Blair was looking like Chicken Little after the sky didn't fall—and since the British citizenry hadn't liked the idea of the war to begin with, they were hopping mad. The Kelly incident would lead to determined and wide-ranging Parliamentary hearings on whether the case for war had been trumped up.

Not so in America. By mid-summer 2003, support for the Iraq adventure had dipped some but not plummeted, despite the rising threat of a long guerrilla war and the fact that no WMD had been found. The White House made it clear it believed nobody really cared about all this "revisionist history."

"The president has moved on," his press secretary, Ari Fleischer, averred. "And, I think, frankly, much of the country has moved on as well." Fleischer added that the idea Iraq's nuclear ambitions had been at the core of its argument for seizing Iraq was "a bunch of bull."

BUT IF THE WHITE HOUSE had moved on, the memo seemingly had not reached everybody. On the first day of June 2003, Bush himself floated his now infamous line on Polish television that WMD had, in fact, been discovered in Iraq. He was referring, apparently, to two odd trailers found the previous month.

"The president is indeed satisfied with the intelligence that he received," Fleischer had said two days earlier. "We have found the bio trucks that can be used only for the purpose of producing biological weapons. That's proof perfect that the intelligence in that regard was right on target."

The idea of mobile labs that could whip up biological weapons was certainly not pleasant, nor was it out of the realm of possibility—in fact, the U.S. was looking for such labs, having been led by some sources to believe that they had, at one time, existed in Iraq. Yet here again, with the discovery of the trailers, the same patterns emerged, showing a complete disregard by the White House for telling the truth, the whole truth, and nothing but the truth: Release the worst-case spin before the facts are in, suppress or ignore expert opinions that don't agree with this scenario, and make the worst-case scenario seem much more threatening than it is.

Thus, while Bush was declaring that his use of intelligence was vindicated by the discovery of two dusty trucks, he failed to note that, a) no traces of chemical or biological weapons were found in them; b) a chorus of weapons experts were already saying the trucks were inappropriate for such use; c) whether or not Hussein had biological weapons in 2003, it was clear he had possessed them in the past and so to find such trailers lying around wouldn't have proven anything in and of itself; and, d) it was unlikely that a trailer that could brew biological weapons was a threat to the United States, as long as it was parked 6,000 miles away in Iraq.

In the end, engineers from the Defense Intelligence Agency, weapons experts from the State Department, and scientists working for British intelligence would agree that the two trailers were most likely used for exactly the purpose Iraq had purported: to produce hydrogen for weather balloons used to target conventional artillery rounds. A British company, Marconi, had sold such trailers to Hussein's regime over 20 years before.

"They are not mobile germ warfare laboratories," said a British biological weapons expert quoted by reporters Peter Beaumont, Antony Barnett, and Gaby Hinsliff in an article in the *Observer* on June 15, 2003. "You could not use them for making biological weapons. They do not even look like them."

The pressure was clearly on to find something, anything. A few weeks after Bush's stumble on Polish television, ex–CIA Director John Deutch remarked that the inability to find chemical or biological weapons in Iraq would be "an intelligence failure of massive proportions." Still the White House was not deterred. On July 24, Vice President Cheney gave a speech in which he cited four statements from the October 2002 National Intelligence Estimate to show how strong he believed the case for Iraqi WMD had been—in stark contrast to what the U.S. search teams were finding on the ground.

"The logical conclusion of Cheney's speech is not the urgency of the Iraqi threat but rather the inescapable reality that 'high confidence' judgments can be dead wrong," pointed out retired CIA veteran Ray McGovern, in a column published July 31, 2003 on AlterNet. "This is often the case when analysts are put under pressure from policymakers, who have already publicly asserted, a priori, the 'correct' answer."

(McGovern knows whereof he speaks. Cofounder of a dissident group of ex-spooks, Veteran Intelligence Professionals for Sanity, he himself chaired National Intelligence Estimates and prepared the president's "Daily Brief" during his 27-year career at the agency.)

But nothing could stop the irrepressible Cheney. In September 2003, he again inexplicably claimed the trailers were weapons labs, without providing any backing for this claim, describing them on NBC's *Meet the Press* as "mobile biological facilities that can be used to produce anthrax or smallpox or whatever else you wanted to use during the course of developing the capacity for an attack."

Nor was the president learning to be any more circumspect. In late

September, he said he believed that Saddam Hussein buried or dispersed his stockpiles of illicit weapons before the United States mounted its invasion in March, but provided no basis for this bold speculation.

IN THE END, NOTHING would be found. Absolutely nothing. As this became clear, the White House tried to shift expectations to finding documents on how to build WMD, or so-called "dual-use" machinery that could be used to manufacture WMD—i.e., equipment that could make both medicine or chemical weapons. Such discoveries, if credible, could be shown to be violations of the UN inspections regime, but they would not prove an imminent threat; they would also imply that as long as inspectors were in the country, Iraq had not expected to get away with any actual weapons production or storage.

One of the odd aspects of the search for WMD after the United States occupied Iraq has been that no UN inspectors, far and away the most knowledgeable experts on Iraq's weapons programs, real or imagined, were allowed into the country despite requests from the UN. In their stead, waves of U.S. inspectors have scoured the country—including a massive 1,400-man Iraq Survey Group that spent 30,000 hours in the field—to no avail.

The White House also made sure that they would have, in charge of this huge investigation, someone highly motivated to find something. David Kay was a former weapons inspector who could be seen regularly on news shows in recent years arguing that Hussein had a substantial and secret stash of WMD; Kay had also publicly called for "a change of regime" in Iraq. Before setting off to Iraq in 2003, he promised, "It's very likely that we will discover remarkable surprises in this enterprise . . . the active deception program is truly amazing once you get inside it."

Amazing, perhaps, but it is unclear what it was hiding. By the end of September 2003, officials acknowledged that one thing Kay was having to look at was whether or not Iraq had been bluffing on a massive scale.

In its October 6 issue, *Time* presented a devastating article based on extensive interviews within the tight-knit community of former administrators, traders, and scientists who had worked on Iraq's WMD programs. The consensus was clear: Not one of those interviewed claimed Iraq had been actively pursuing chemical, biological, or nuclear weapons in recent years.

> Saddam's henchmen all make essentially the same claim: that Iraq's once massive unconventional-weapons program was destroyed or dismantled in the 1990s and never rebuilt; that officials destroyed or never kept the documents that would prove it; that the shell games Saddam played with UN inspectors were designed to conceal his progress on conventional weapons systems—missiles, air defenses, radar—not biological or chemical programs; and that even Saddam . . . may not have known what he actually had or, more to the point, didn't have. It would be an irony almost too much to bear to consider that he doomed his country to war because he was intent on protecting weapons systems that didn't exist in the first place.

Unfortunately, the United States has granted its inspection team a budget that may soar to $600 million—compare this to the United Nations inspectors' annual budget of $60 million—and placed it in the hands of a man who is, in the words of the Carnegie Foundation for Peace's Joseph Cirincione, "both salesman and fact-finder for the administration." This clear conflict of interest is distorting his analysis of the data, as Cirincione wrote on Oct. 2, 2003:

> Buried in the October 2 congressional testimony of David Kay were two bombshells: all the Iraq Survey Group evidence collected to date indicates that there were not any active programs to develop or produce chemical or nuclear weapons.
> In the middle of a paragraph halfway through his testimony,

Kay presents what should have been his lead finding: "Information found to date suggests that Iraq's large-scale capability to develop, produce, and fill new CW munitions was reduced—if not entirely destroyed—during Operations Desert Storm and Desert Fox, 13 years of UN sanctions, and UN inspections." Similarly, three paragraphs into Kay's description of Saddam's intention to develop nuclear weapons, he says: "To date we have not uncovered evidence that Iraq undertook significant post–1998 steps to actually build nuclear weapons or produce fissile material."

It is understandable that Mr. Kay did not wish to highlight these findings. They are not mentioned in his concluding points, nor in his opening summary. They directly refute the two main charges of administration officials before the war as well as the claim that UN inspections were not working. It now appears from everything we have been able to learn since the war that the combination of UN sanctions, inspections, and the military strikes of 1991 and 1998 effectively destroyed Iraq's chemical and nuclear weapons programs and prevented their reconstruction. The same appears to be true for the biological weapons program and the missile program. . . .

Once again, the truth about the threat Iraq posed to the world had been politicized by our government beyond all recognition.

THIRD LIE

Iraq's Nuclear Weapons

"The British government has learned that Saddam Hussein recently sought significant quantities of uranium from Africa."

—President Bush, January 28, 2003, State of the Union address

"That information was erroneous, and they knew about it well ahead of both the publication of the British White Paper and the president's State of the Union address."

—Ambassador Joe Wilson, July 6, 2003, on *Meet the Press*

"How does it feel to be the baboon that threw the turd that hit the target and finally stuck?"

—Unidentified friend of Joe Wilson, as relayed by Wilson in August 2003

BY THE TIME Ambassador Joseph C. Wilson, the last American official to formally talk to Saddam Hussein, walked onto the world's highest stage carrying a big torch, the accumulation of political kindling had piled quite high. The lies of the White House were being exposed daily in the alternative and foreign presses, and no WMD were being found in now completely occupied Iraq, but the establishment press seemed to have little desire to light the fire.

Responding to a request from Vice President Cheney's office—which was aggressively proactive about digging up dirt on Iraq, as we shall see—the CIA had dispatched Wilson in February 2002 to the country of

Niger for eight days to investigate the claim of an attempted uranium ore sale to Iraq. A charismatic man with decades of diplomatic experience in Africa and the Middle East, Wilson worked his old contacts in the country to get to the bottom of the story.

His finding? The allegations were "bogus and unrealistic," he says he told the CIA conclusively upon his return. There was simply no merit to them. His report to the CIA was verbal, but he knew it was standard operating procedure for the officers present to file reports generated from the debriefing; an answer given to Cheney in either oral or written form; and reports to be sent back by the U.S. Embassy and the ambassador in Niger.

Imagine Wilson's shock, then, when *a year later* he would find this same claim of African uranium purchases mentioned in Bush's State of the Union address of January 28, 2003, in what became known to pundits as the "16 words": "The British government has learned that Saddam Hussein recently sought significant quantities of uranium from Africa." Despite calling it "British intelligence," it was based on the same story Wilson had investigated—and which the White House and CIA had omitted from a speech three months earlier because it had been discredited.

Sparks flew a couple months later in March when the International Atomic Energy Agency—after months of being denied access to them—announced that the Niger documents were obvious and clumsy forgeries, full of telltale inaccuracies that betrayed the fact that whoever created them (still unknown) didn't know jack about Niger. A week after the IAEA's bombshell, Senator Jay Rockefeller (D-WV) formally asked for an FBI investigation into the matter, stating that "the fabrication of these documents may be part of a larger deception aimed at manipulating public opinion . . . regarding Iraq."

Cheney said the IAEA was "frankly, wrong," however, and Colin Powell merely demurred that the documents were offered in "good faith." The woodpile was giving off smoke, but hadn't yet caught fire: We were still talking about whether the basic intelligence was good or bad, rather than whether it had been misrepresented knowingly.

For his part, Wilson was an unlikely candidate to throw on some kerosene. A slick and confident man, every bit the former ambassador, he had been a key organizer of President Clinton's historic tour of Africa. Going public with his investigation of the Niger uranium would give Wilson a notoriety that could endanger his career, his reputation, and, as we shall see, even his family. But as he likes to joke, he wasn't scared to take on Bush's intimidating chief strategist, Karl Rove, since he had sat face-to-face across from Saddam Hussein in tense negotiations while the top-ranking U.S. diplomat in Baghdad at the time of Gulf War I. In that role, he was called a hero by former President Bush.

After several appearances as an unnamed source in news reports in preceding months, he wrote a column under his name in the *New York Times* on July 6, 2003 that told his side of the story in no uncertain terms. "Based on my experience with the administration in the months leading up to the war, I have little choice but to conclude that some of the intelligence related to Iraq's nuclear weapons program was twisted to exaggerate the Iraqi threat," he wrote.

The fire had been lit, and soon the establishment media decided to fan it. For several weeks in the summer of 2003, the "16 words" became front-page news, even penetrating the strange world of cable news shows and landing on the cover of the big newsweeklies. It didn't help Bush that the controversy broke at the same time that it was becoming increasingly clear even to Donald Rumsfeld that the United States was facing an ongoing, organized guerrilla war and Iraq was still wallowing in a grim state of postwar anarchy.

The cover headlines of *Time* for July 21 summed up the combination perfectly: *"Untruth & Consequences: How Flawed Was the Case for Going to War Against Saddam?"* was splayed over a picture of Bush giving the State of the Union, while *"Plus: An Intimate Look at Seven American Soldiers Who Died this Month in Iraq"* referred to a series of wrenching portraits of regular people of various ages and background who had sacrificed their lives for a questionable cause.

The Bush White House, never one for mea culpas, was forced to respond with a sort of apology. "With the advantage of hindsight, it's known now what was not known by the White House prior to the speech. This information should not have risen to the level of a presidential speech," said Bush Press Secretary Ari Fleischer three days after Wilson's op-ed.

Yet, in a position echoing that of embattled British Prime Minister Tony Blair, an unnamed White House official told the *Washington Post* that same week that the Niger documents were "only one piece of evidence in a larger body of evidence suggesting Iraq attempted to purchase uranium from Africa." None of this "larger body of evidence" has ever been produced, however.

Condoleezza Rice, too, tried to argue that this was all much ado about nothing. "Of course, it was information that was mistaken," she said on June 8, 2003. "But it was a relatively small part of the case about nuclear weapons and nuclear reconstitution." Yet, as we shall see, it was one of very few pieces of intelligence, none of which would hold up, that the administration produced to bolster its argument that Hussein was close to getting nukes.

"If it was only a small piece and not terribly significant then I don't see why the president would do what's very unusual, which is to declassify sensitive information and announce it to the world," Thielmann told Bill Moyers, responding to Rice's quote. "You don't do that casually."

In subsequent weeks, the White House's attempts to scapegoat the CIA's Tenet and Rice's aides "in the bowels of the bureaucracy"—would backfire, and Bush began to look politically vulnerable for the first time since 9/11. Things took an even nastier turn when somebody at the White House, it seems, attempted to "out" Joe Wilson's wife as an undercover CIA agent by leaking the allegation to conservative pundit Robert Novak, blowing her cover and possibly endangering her work or even her life. (This would later spawn a Justice Department investigation and calls in Congress for a special prosecutor.)

Finally, Bush retreated, accepting, without too much enthusiasm, responsibility for the State of the Union falsehood: "I take personal responsibility for everything I say, of course. Absolutely. I also take responsibility for making decisions on war and peace. And I analyzed a thorough body of intelligence—good, solid, sound intelligence—that led me to come to the conclusion that it was necessary to remove Saddam Hussein from power."

Whether he was sincere or not in this half-hearted apology, the story began to die out. And while Bush had taken some real hits to his image as a "straight shooter" and a few establishment journalists, such as the *Post*'s Walter Pincus, had begun to document the overall pattern of distortion of which the uranium tale was just a tiny part, most of the media moved on to safer, less politicized stories.

Also missed in the hullabaloo was the fact that the uranium angle was a complete red herring from the start: Iraq already possessed stores of uranium similar to what it was alleged to want to buy from Niger, and a new shipment wouldn't have put them any closer to having nuclear weapons. To process any uranium to weapons grade, they would have had to run hundreds of gas centrifuges created specifically for that purpose, and these centrifuges would give off telltale gases, heat, and gamma radiation which can be detected by electronic surveillance tools.

The State Department's intelligence agency, the INR, in a footnote in the National Intelligence Estimate on Iraq for 2002, expressed this forcefully. Having allowed that Hussein wanted nukes and "is pursuing at least a limited effort to maintain and acquire nuclear weapon–related capabilities," it concluded that none of it amounted to much: "The activities we have detected do not, however, add up to a compelling case that Iraq is currently pursuing what INR would consider to be an integrated and comprehensive approach to acquire nuclear weapons. Iraq may be doing so, but INR considers the available evidence inadequate to support such a judgment."

In July 2003, it would be revealed by the *Washington Post* and others that the CIA's chief had, in fact, warned in writing to Deputy National Security Advisor Stephen Hadley and Bush's chief speechwriter, Michael Gerson, on October 5 and 6, 2002—three months before Bush's State of the Union address in which the 16 words appeared— that the agency had strong doubts about the Niger claim. The allegations, said the memos, were built on weak evidence, were not particularly significant, and assumed Iraq was pursuing an acquisition that was arguably not possible and of questionable value because Iraq had its own supplies.

The idea that the Niger tale just sort of fell into the State of the Union speech by accident was further undermined when the *New Yorker's* Seymour Hersh wrote that the very same day Blair unveiled this alleged "smoking gun," CIA Director George Tenet was scaring the Senate Foreign Relations Committee with the supposed Niger-Iraq link, in advance of the vote on authorization of force against Iraq.

Coincidence? Possibly. But it seemed much more likely the decision to release certain bits of secret intelligence was being made on a careful, case-by-case basis as part of the joint British-U.S. propaganda campaign. In the end, the only logical assumption is that the White House officials who approved this and similarly phony claims about Iraq's WMD were taking a calculated risk: Push well past the edges of the truth envelope in our campaign for war and postpone any potential fallout in negative public opinion until later, after we've taken Iraq—and, presumably, been recognized as glorious liberators.

■ ■ ■

"After three months of intrusive inspections, we have, to date, found no evidence or plausible indication of the revival of a nuclear weapons program in Iraq."

—International Atomic Energy Agency report, March 7, 2003

"We believe [Saddam] has, in fact, reconstituted nuclear weapons."

—Vice President Dick Cheney on March 16, 2003, on *Meet the Press*

"Yeah, I did misspeak. . . . We never had any evidence that [Hussein] had acquired a nuclear weapon."

—Vice President Dick Cheney on September 14, 2003, on *Meet the Press*

THERE ARE MANY HEINOUS tools for violence that have been created or employed by our innovative species, but there is only one true weapon of targeted mass destruction: the nuclear bomb. If mustard gas or anthrax are WMD, then nukes are WMMMMMD.

It was almost 60 years ago when two tiny American nukes killed some 200,000 people in Hiroshima and Nagasaki. Today, nine countries possess a combined 31,000 nuclear weapons: the United States, Russia, China, France, Britain, Israel, Pakistan, India, and, possibly, North Korea, which the United States says has one or two (as well as dozens of missiles capable of hitting Japan or South Korea). Pakistan and India, involved in a seemingly endless low-grade border war, possess enough plutonium between them for 75 to 150 nuclear bombs, according to *Scientific American*. Israel, surrounded by enemies, has between 100 and 200 nuclear warheads.

Iraq, it has been discovered at great cost in American lives and money, has none. According to the president, however, it was worth the price of admission to see Saddam Hussein's poker hand. "The first time we may be completely certain he has nuclear weapons is when, God forbids, he uses one," Bush told the United Nations General Assembly on September 12, 2002. "We owe it to all our citizens to do everything in our power to prevent that day from coming."

On July 24, 2003, with the administration on the defensive as day after day went by with no WMD discoveries in occupied Iraq, Vice

President Cheney defended the administration's prewar insistence that Iraq was very close to getting nukes.

"The intelligence community also had high confidence in the judgment that—and I quote [from the National Intelligence Estimate]: 'Iraq could make a nuclear weapon in months to a year once it acquires sufficient weapons-grade fissile material.' End quote. Well, ladies and gentlemen, this is some of what we knew. Knowing these things, how could we, I ask, have allowed that threat to stand?"

This sure sounded scary. Yet, any moderately industrialized nation could, once it "acquires sufficient weapons-grade fissile material," build a basic nuclear weapon rather quickly. The science to do so is in the public domain, and the technical specs are manageable. It is precisely the weapons-grade fissile material that Iraq didn't have, and the inspectors from the International Atomic Energy Agency had said as much in their reports running right up to a few days before the invasion.

Moreover, the U.S. document Cheney was citing was compiled half a year before the IAEA announced its conclusions, which directly rebuked the NIE's conclusions. Remember, too, that the IAEA inspectors were supposed to have access to any relevant U.S. intelligence that would have proved otherwise.

"I hope the U.S. does not know anything we do not know," the IAEA chief inspector, Mohamed ElBaradei, had told *Time* back in January. "If they do, they should tell us. If they are talking about indigenous capability, Iraq is far away from that. If Iraq has imported material hidden, then you're talking about six months or a year. But that's a big if."

Nine days after the IAEA made ElBaradei's definitive assessment public, there was Cheney telling Tim Russert on *Meet the Press* that Iraq had "reconstituted" nuclear weapons, a badly exaggerated echo of what the outdated NIE had surmised. Either ElBaradei or Cheney was talking through his hat—or simply lying. But why? Weren't both men on the same team?

In reality, the inspectors and the Bush White House had always been at odds because their goals were very different. The UN and IAEA's mandate was to the disarm Iraq, while the White House wanted a convincing rationale for a preemptive strike. A disarmed Iraq would actually pose a problem for Bush, since he had already committed to the invasion and needed to keep his rationales lined up.

If the IAEA had doctored its reports the way some of the U.S. intelligence agencies had, to make Hussein seem on the cusp of possessing nukes, then it would have gotten along fine with the White House. As it was, however, the guys on Pennsylvania Avenue could barely say the word "inspectors" without spitting on the ground and grinding it with the points of their wingtips.

Of course, forced to choose between the president of the United States and a bunch of foreign experts, Americans didn't hesitate (although they did make it clear in poll after poll that they wanted the UN to give its seal of approval to the war). And why shouldn't they? After all, Bush's intelligence forces have a budget that in 1998 was estimated by the federal government at an aggregate $26.7 billion annually—they should know what they are talking about, right?

Not necessarily. In fact, the evidence that allegedly showed Iraq was actively pursuing nukes had been crumbling all fall and winter, leaving the White House and Britain to rely on flimsier and flimsier "facts." This is why the Bush team took what in hindsight was a perversely risky decision to use questionable if not completely discredited intelligence snippets in such scrutinized speeches as the State of the Union address.

After the war, *Washington Post* staff writer Walter Pincus described in a July 16 article the bind the administration had found itself in by the time of the State of the Union speech to Congress and the nation: "[A] review of speeches and reports, plus interviews with present and former administration officials and intelligence analysts, suggests that between October 7, when President Bush made a speech laying out the case for military action against Hussein, and January 28, when he gave his State of the Union address, almost all the other evidence had either been undercut or disproved by UN inspectors in Iraq."

Unfortunately, if Hussein was going to properly play the role of a comic book villain as a foil to American purity, he had to have The Ultimate Weapon and be pointing it at us. The narrative Bush was dedicated to demanded it and, apparently, was not up for discussion. At the moment when prudence would have suggested the White House back off the nuke claims, it kept sending out an elephant of an argument walking on the spindliest of giraffe legs.

Eventually, the beast would collapse—but not before helping to convince us to support sending hundreds of thousand of troops into battle. Let's go back and see what happened along the way.

SADDAM HUSSEIN'S IRAQ was a wanna-be nation, trying fitfully for decades to follow Israel, Pakistan, China, and India into an atomic club presumed to grant great nationalist prestige to its members.

"The [2003] Iraq War was the first application of the new theory that preventive war can be an effective instrument against the spread of nuclear, biological, and chemical weapons," wrote Joseph Cirincione in the July/August 2003 issue of *Foreign Policy*. "'Prevention' invites a medical metaphor. And, indeed, observers often imagine an epidemic when they think of weapons of mass destruction proliferation. Yet the best metaphor for proliferation is a cancer that results from environmental causes and metastasizes in predictable patterns from cell to neighboring cell. China gets nuclear weapons, India responds to China, and then Pakistan to India. Israel builds nuclear weapons, then Iraq tries, along with Iran, even as the acquisition of chemical and biological weapons by other states adds to the region-wide malignancy. North Korea's nuclear weapons program prompts worries of proliferation to Japan and South Korea, and so on."

There have been many failed attempts since WWII to halt the proliferation of nuclear weapons, North Korea being a striking example. However, after two decades of Israeli and U.S. air strikes, wars with Iran and the United States, and UN sanctions and inspectors, Iraq was actually a terrific example of the potential effectiveness of what is usually called "containment"—pressure applied to keep a global menace in check without pursuing outright war.

In fact, Secretary of State Colin Powell himself vigorously defended the containment policy in Egypt on February 24, 2001:

> [T]he sanctions exist—not for the purpose of hurting the Iraqi people, but for the purpose of keeping in check Saddam Hussein's ambitions toward developing weapons of mass destruction. We should constantly be reviewing our policies, constantly be looking at those sanctions to make sure that they are directed toward that purpose. That purpose is every bit as important now as it was 10 years ago when we began it. *And frankly they have worked. He has not developed any significant capability with respect to weapons of mass destruction.* He is unable to project conventional power against his neighbors. So in effect, our policies have strengthened the security of the neighbors of Iraq, and these are policies that we are going to keep in place, but we are always willing to review them to make sure that they are being carried out in a way that does not affect the Iraqi people but does affect the Iraqi regime's ambitions and their ability to acquire weapons of mass destruction. [Italics added]

Before the first Gulf War, Iraq reportedly had been quite close to producing a crude, Hiroshima-sized atomic weapon that could be lobbed at Israel using a Scud missile of Soviet design. Of course, it would have been absolute suicide to nuke Israel, considering the unprecedented striking power of its key ally, the United States. Hussein likely hoped that if he could brandish a nuke, the world might choose to overlook his subsequent seizure of Kuwait.

In any case, he ran out of time, and his nuclear program was effectively dismantled between 1991 and 1995 by inspectors working under international agreements which Iraq was forced to make after its defeat. His highly enriched uranium was sent to Russia and his less enriched stockpiles were put under seal inside the country by the International Atomic Energy Agency, subject to annual inspections.

By January 2003, not only had martial Iraq been prevented from making war for more than a decade, but its nuclear program was now basically back at square one, retaining some of its scientists and dual-use machinery but lacking any weapons-grade uranium or plutonium. Until Dick Cheney inexplicably said it on *Meet the Press* just before the war, not even the most rabid hawks claimed Hussein possessed working nuclear weapons, estimating only that he could be months or years away from such a capability depending on whether he was able to import weapons-grade nuclear materiel or was forced to develop it himself.

Furthermore, before "Operation Iraqi Freedom" was launched, it was not actually clear if Hussein was still actively pursuing his dreams of being a nuclear-powered dictator or just wanted to keep his enemies on their toes. This became even fuzzier in the war's aftermath, as we saw in the previous chapter. But let's assume for argument's sake that since he had wanted nukes in the past, and being nothing if not stubborn, truculent, and power-mad, Hussein was still working feverishly to secretly build the capability to do so.

The White House certainly claimed to believe this. "Delegates to the General Assembly, we have been more than patient," President Bush told the United Nations on September 12, 2002. "We've tried sanctions. We've tried the carrot of oil for food, and the stick of coalition military strikes. But Saddam Hussein has defied all these efforts and continues to develop weapons of mass destruction."

For Bush, the answer was clear. According to documents marked "secret" and prepared for the Joint Chiefs of Staff in 2003 (and leaked to the *Washington Times* in early September of that year), on August 29, 2002—two weeks before his UN address—Bush had signed off on the plan to invade, occupy, and "reconstruct" Iraq. Invade Iraq, the thinking went, and we could destroy the country's alleged nukes program once and for all.

According to the National Intelligence Estimate on Iraq made in the fall of 2002 by the United States' combined intelligence agencies, the only scenario in which it was deemed likely that Hussein might choose to use nuclear weapons (or give them to others) was if the United States invaded. This of course made sense, since countries want nukes to deter their foes from attacking them.

It also went a long way toward explaining the stark contrast between U.S. intelligence agencies' calm assessment of Iraq's modest military threat and the shrill hysteria of the White House's translation of the available intelligence.

Whether sending the U.S. military overseas to overthrow Hussein was a cynical political ploy to turn Bush from whelp to warrior, or a simple grab for oil, a question still remained: What was the rush? After all, as we have seen, Iraq's conventional forces and biological and chemical weapons were less imposing than they had been in decades. Its closest neighbors professed no fear of the once formidable "Baghdad tiger." Why did Bush so heavily front-load his investment in invasion—sending troops before he signed up allies, for example—if there was no pressing need to do so?

"I think it would be a mistake to focus on the issue of weapons of mass destruction," influential ex–State Department official Charles Duelfer told former weapons inspector Scott Ritter, as related in Ritter's book *Endgame*. "To do so ignores the larger issue of whether or not we want this dictator [Saddam Hussein] to have control over a nation capable of producing six million barrels of oil a day. We simply cannot allow Iraq to have that kind of power and influence."

For many of these architects of American foreign policy, even a militarily neutered Baghdad regime would be unacceptably independent.

"If you focus on the weapons issue, then the first thing you know, Iraq will be given a clean bill of health, sanctions will be lifted, and then

Iraq will, at the first excuse, kick the inspectors out," Duelfer said. "We will be left having no leverage over Iraq or how Saddam chooses to spend his money."

There is a corollary to this, as well, looking through the other side of the glass; namely, that if you want to prevent a U.S. invasion, nukes may be the only way to go. As the Carnegie Endowment for International Peace's Cirincione writes, "To be an effective treatment for proliferation, preventive war must not only remove the direct threat, it must also dissuade would-be proliferators. The United States and other concerned states may yet try to use the Iraq treatment as an object lesson to induce states such as North Korea and Iran to change their behavior. But the early signs are that these regimes have drawn an opposite conclusion . . . Like India's army chief of staff after the first Iraq war, officials in Pyongyang and Tehran may believe that if one day you find yourself opposed by the United States, you'd better have a nuclear weapon."

All of this helps us understand why the United States so severely denigrated the inspectors, with Rumsfeld and Cheney calling them "ineffective" and a "waste of time."

This kind of public abuse was unprecedented, especially considering that because of the U.S. buildup of troops, Iraq was going to once again let inspectors in. Cheney was unmoved by voices of moderation—or the avowed pro-inspections policy of the United States—arguing that the return of UN weapons inspectors to Iraq would only strengthen Hussein.

Later, when Iraq was acquiescing to a series of the inspectors' demands and missiles deemed to have excessive range were being destroyed on an almost daily basis by the UN, the United States decided it could not wait another month to begin the invasion. "One can hardly avoid the impression that, after a period of somewhat reluctant cooperation, there has been an acceleration of initiatives from the Iraqi side since the end of January," Hans Blix, the chief of the UN inspectors, told the Security Council on March 7, 2003, although he cautioned that Iraq had not cooperated "immediately, unconditionally, and actively"—no shocker there.

Blix went on to cite increased air surveillance using U.S., French, German, and Russian planes, the unfettered ability "to perform professional no-notice inspections all over Iraq," rising cooperation on private interviews with scientists, inspections of "mobile units," destruction of 40 percent of the Al-Samoud 2 missile cache, and excavation and analysis of a major weapons disposal site.

Most important, Blix noted that for the UN to finish its survey of sites, documents, and relevant people, it "will not take years, nor weeks, but months." In the meantime, he emphasized, "we are not watching the breaking of toothpicks. Lethal weapons are being destroyed." On the nuclear question, the International Atomic Energy Agency had already announced it had "found no evidence or plausible indication of the revival of a nuclear weapons program in Iraq."

This was no less than a complete rejuvenation of the inspections regime which had crumbled in 1998. Yet, the White House was clearly not happy about it—despite the fact it could have taken credit for the inspectors' new victories, because they clearly had something to do with the 200,000-plus troops the United States had shipped to the Persian Gulf by then.

But why not? What was the rush? Couldn't the inspectors be given another four months—the time they said it would take to complete their work? Wouldn't keeping the troops in readiness still be much cheaper than actually fighting a war and then rebuilding a country you'd just destroyed?

Some in the media speculated that the Pentagon was impatient to launch the assault before temperatures soared in the Iraqi hot season. Others pointed out that it would be politically awkward to bring all those troops home if it meant leaving Hussein in power. These were not the reasons provided by the president, however, in a national address on March 6, 2003:

We have arrived at an important moment in confronting the threat posed to our nation and to peace by Saddam Hussein and his weapons of terror. Saddam Hussein has a long history of reckless aggression and terrible crimes. He possesses weapons of terror. He provides funding and training and safe haven to terrorists—terrorists who would willingly use weapons of mass destruction against America and other peace-loving countries. Saddam Hussein and his weapons are a direct threat to this country, to our people, and to all free people.

If the world fails to confront the threat posed by the Iraqi regime, refusing to use force, even as a last resort, free nations would assume immense and unacceptable risks. The attacks of September the 11th, 2001 showed what the enemies of America did with four airplanes. We will not wait to see what terrorists or terrorist states could do with weapons of mass destruction.

We are determined to confront threats wherever they arise. I will not leave the American people at the mercy of the Iraqi dictator and his weapons.

Like an action movie director who always cuts to shots of the ticking time bomb, Bush and his top staff were relentless in stressing repeatedly that the clock was running out and the United States had to act now. Never mind that with inspectors crawling all over his country, Hussein was not in any position to advance his weapons programs.

After the war, many pundits expressed surprise that no nuclear weapons program was found in Iraq. But if they had been closely following the series of phony or trumped-up facts the White House had been pushing to prove this—and that were exposed before the war began—they would have seen it coming. Let's look at the biggest ones.

■ ■ ■

"Lacking persuasive evidence that Baghdad has launched a coherent effort to reconstitute its nuclear weapons program, INR is unwilling to speculate that such an effort began soon after the departure of UN inspectors or to project a timeline for the completion of activities it does not now see happening."

—From the 2002 National Intelligence Estimate on Iraq. INR is the State Department's internal intelligence agency

"The evidence indicates that Iraq is reconstituting its nuclear weapons program. . . . Iraq has attempted to purchase high-strength aluminum tubes and other equipment needed for gas centrifuges, which are used to enrich uranium for nuclear weapons."

—President Bush, October 7, 2002, in a speech in Cincinnati

ON SEPTEMBER 8, 2002, in a classic example of how easy it is for the White House to manipulate the media, and thus the public, the *New York Times* ran a story planted by the Bush administration. The front-page article, written by Judith Miller and Michael Gordon and headlined *"U.S. Says Hussein Intensifies Quest for A-Bomb Parts,"* informed Americans that, according to unnamed Bush officials, Iraq had repeatedly attempted to secretly purchase aluminum tubes "specially designed" for enriching uranium as part of a nuclear weapons program based on their "diameter, thickness, and other technical properties."

It was the ultimate advertorial: great placement, perfect message, excellent timing—all basically controlled by the advertiser but looking as if it was coming from "neutral" sources. From its August launch through its acceptance by Congress in October, the Bush marketing campaign for the war was perfectly executed, and the tubes revelation was a classic example.

By the time the truth that the attempted purchases were neither secret nor likely intended for nuclear uses was tracked down and exposed by whistle-blowers, journalists, and the International Atomic Energy Agency, it wouldn't matter, having already served dutifully as a scary totem in Bush speech after Bush speech. When its power did flag, it would simply be replaced by another shaky fact put into the rotation and foisted upon a compliant media. This leak-and-retreat tactic proved astonishingly effective up to and through the war.

One key to a president exploiting shaky yet convenient intelligence data is to always maintain deniability. Aiding and abetting this is the array of different intelligence agencies that the president has reporting to him—CIA, NSA, FBI, and sub-agencies of State, Defense, and so on—not to mention the information generated by allied nations' intelligence agencies that are passed along (more on that later). Combined, these agencies, each with their own strong institutional biases and rivalries, generate so much data that it is child's play for politicians (or reporters with good sources) to cherry-pick opinions that fit their policy platform (or story angle).

In an effort to control this kind of chicanery, the intelligence agencies are often required to pool their insights and evidence into overview documents to see whether or not there is a consensus as to their reliability. Relevant experts may also be called in, especially in a case like this where highly technical expertise was essential to separating fact from fiction.

Thus, when it was revealed to the public by the president that the aluminum tubes in question could (and likely would) be used to refine uranium, one would assume he was so confident in the assertion because of just such an expert intelligence consensus. In fact, as we shall see, nothing could have been further from the truth.

First, some background: Uranium enrichment is a critical step in transforming natural uranium into nuclear fuel, whether for peaceful uses or bomb-building. The ore is ground, treated, and converted into a gas, which is then pumped into the centrifuge that rotates at twice the speed of sound. The heavier of the two isotopes, uranium-238, is drawn against the sides of the centrifuge cylinder, separating it from the lighter uranium-235, the desired end product. The uranium passes through hundreds of centrifuges, each with a six-foot cylinder at its core, in order to refine it still further.

When the experts looked at the tubes later cited by the White House, however, questions immediately arose over whether they were appropriate for such centrifuges. Working under a blanket of enormous pressure coming from the White House, and especially the vice president, to find damning things regarding Iraq and nuclear weapons, a full-blown row soon broke out within the alphabet soup of U.S. intelligence agencies over this obscure issue.

For their part, CIA and the Defense Intelligence Agency believed the tubes were similar to those used in Iraq's previous attempt to build nukes, while the State Department's INR and the Department of Energy were adamant that they were in fact much more appropriate for artillery shells. The division was made explicit in the 2002 NIE report on Saddam's pursuit of WMD, as the State Department experts insisted a sharply worded dissent be included in the overall report, controlled by the top dog in the intelligence "community," the CIA.

Here's what the NIE said: "Most agencies believe that Saddam's personal interest in and Iraq's aggressive attempts to obtain high-strength aluminum tubes for centrifuge rotors . . . provide compelling evidence that Saddam is reconstituting a uranium enrichment effort for Baghdad's nuclear weapons program."

Here's the INR dissent:

> In INR's view Iraq's efforts to acquire aluminum tubes is central to the argument that Baghdad is reconstituting its nuclear weapons program, but INR is not persuaded that the tubes in question are intended for use as centrifuge rotors. INR accepts the judgment of technical experts at the U.S. Department of Energy (DOE) who have concluded that the tubes Iraq seeks to

acquire are poorly suited for use in gas centrifuges to be used for uranium enrichment and finds unpersuasive the arguments advanced by others to make the case that they are intended for that purpose. INR considers it far more likely that the tubes are intended for another purpose, most likely the production of artillery rockets.

The very large quantities being sought, the way the tubes were tested by the Iraqis, and the atypical lack of attention to operational security in the procurement efforts are among the factors, in addition to the DOE assessment, that lead INR to conclude that the tubes are not intended for use in Iraq's nuclear weapons program.

Newsweek later revealed that the tubes order had actually been posted on the Internet, and was thus not a secret procurement at all.

Meanwhile, British experts weighed in against the White House's interpretation and some CIA analysts also expressed doubts. A side debate raged as to whether the tubes, if they were not originally fit for use in the right centrifuges, could be machined to the right specs, but again there was only heated debate rather than consensus. In July, the United States had intercepted one shipment and obtained a tube; it was coated with a protective chemical that would have had to be removed if it were to be put to a nuclear purpose.

Remember, all of this arguing happened three months before the *New York Times* story and before Bush and his ministers began referencing it prominently all over the place. And the longer the tubes bounced around the intelligence community, the iffier it got as a piece of evidence affirming Iraq's threat to the world.

According to the groundbreaking investigative article by John B. Judis and Spencer Ackerman which appeared in the June 30 issue of the *New Republic* and relied on a slew of intelligence sources, it was the critics of the more sinister interpretation of the tubes' purpose who had really done their homework while the CIA had been quick to make a snap judgment from which it would not budge. They also pointed out that the debunkers at the DOE were the true experts in processing uranium.

"The tubes' thick walls and particular diameter made them a poor fit for uranium enrichment, even after modification," wrote Judis and Ackerman. Yet, the CIA and DIA "clung so tenaciously to this point of view about it being a nuclear weapons program when the evidence just became clearer and clearer over time that it wasn't the case," a participant in the inter-agency dispute told them.

To make matters worse, at least one expert felt the whole squabble was being dealt with very strangely. "I was told that this dispute had not been mediated by a competent, impartial, technical committee, as it should have been according to accepted practice," David Albright of the Institute for Science and International Security wrote on his organization's website in March 2003.

Ultimately, the CIA, as the top intelligence agency, won out, forcing their analysis into the NIE. And on September 8, 2002, the *New York Times* front page trumpeted its scoop, announcing that Iraq had "embarked on a worldwide hunt for materials to make an atomic bomb" by trying to purchase "specially designed aluminum tubes" that unidentified Bush administration sources said could be used to make centrifuges to enrich uranium. Unnamed Bush officials specifically cited the "diameter, thickness, and other technical properties" of the tubes as evidence of their appropriateness for centrifuge use, without acknowledging that this was the source of great expert controversy.

But the battle wouldn't end there. The *New Republic's* investigation the following spring found many of the tube skeptics still hopping mad, incited by the continued use of the centrifuge claim. One intelligence analyst, who was part of the internal multi-agency tubes investigation, angrily—though anonymously—told the magazine known for its hawkish stances, "You had senior American officials like Condoleezza Rice saying the only use of this aluminum really is uranium centrifuges. She said that on television. And that's just a lie."

And Rice hadn't stopped there. After saying on the September 8, 2002 *Late Edition* that the tubes "are only really suited for nuclear weapons programs, centrifuge programs," she then went on to brandish the ultimate image of twentieth century terror: "The problem here is that there will always be some uncertainty about how quickly [Hussein] can acquire nuclear weapons, but we don't want the smoking gun to be a mushroom cloud."

Rice also took a dig at the inspectors, as other White House officials did consistently throughout the walk-up to the war. Apparently not intimidated, however, the International Atomic Energy Agency was blunt in its assessment of the tubes. On January 24, ElBaradei told the *Washington Post,* "It may be technically possible that the tubes could be used to enrich uranium, but you'd have to believe that Iraq deliberately ordered the wrong stock and intended to spend a great deal of time and money reworking each piece." And on March 7, the IAEA stated its analysis quite clearly in its formal report to the United Nations:

"With regard to the aluminum tubes, the IAEA has conducted a thorough investigation of Iraq's attempt to purchase large quantities of high-strength aluminum tubes. As previously reported, Iraq has maintained that these aluminum tubes were sold for rocket production. Extensive field investigation and document analysis have failed to uncover any evidence that Iraq intended to use these 81-millimeter tubes for any project other than the reverse engineering of rockets."

It took exactly six months to get from the *New York Times* front-page story to this expert denunciation of the claim. In two weeks, the war to "disarm Saddam Hussein" would begin.

IT WASN'T UNTIL THE summer of 2003 that the mainstream media, emboldened by the fact that Americans were still dying in Iraq in what seemed an increasingly Vietnam-like scenario, began to belatedly raise questions about the administration's shaky case for war.

Specifically, with the emergence of former ambassador–turned whistleblower Joe Wilson, it now focused like a laser on the infamous "16 words" in Bush's 2003 State of the Union speech, which, as we have seen, described an alleged attempted purchase of uranium from Africa that had already been debunked by the CIA and would later be demolished by the IAEA.

In fact, it appeared to be little more than a throwaway line, and Bush had even left an out for himself—crediting the intelligence to the Brits. Yet this would be the one that finally got Bush in trouble, because it gave the media a "gotcha" to grab onto.

However, for those who had been watching the administration's modus operandi since the launch of its attempt to mobilize support for "regime change" in Iraq, what some called "yellowcake-gate" was simply a particularly sloppy version of the same game it had been playing with the facts since the previous fall: Use scary words, cherry-pick the intelligence that fits your argument, and exploit people's areas of ignorance and short attention span.

Similar to his use of the opaque term "weapons of mass destruction," Bush brandished the loaded word "uranium." As with the aluminum tubes, he completely ignored the fact that those within the U.S. intelligence establishment who were best placed to analyze the evidence had come to conclusions directly opposite of those he was presenting to the American people. And he once again played upon our ignorance of technical or scientific details to create the impression of a smoking gun where none existed.

The White House continued to be hell-bent on supersizing our fear, turning an admittedly scary world into a chamber of horrors. And it worked: Americans came to believe Hussein had nukes, or at least was well on his way to making them. An ABC News poll published on December 17, 2002 said a full 89 percent of Americans believed Iraq "does possess chemical, biological, or nuclear weapons."

However, according to the United States' own consensus, the National Intelligence Estimate, Hussein wanted nukes but didn't currently have a functioning nuclear weapons program that could build them. It held out two ways he could get them, and guesstimated when he could have them in each highly speculative scenario.

In the first scenario, "If Baghdad acquires sufficient fissile material from abroad it could make a nuclear weapon within several months to a year." Translation: If Iraq is able to buy enough plutonium or weapons-grade enriched uranium on the black market, it could probably jerry-rig a nuclear bomb. (It should be pointed out that this is true for many of the "rogue nations" on the world stage, since knowing how to actually build a nuclear bomb is not much of a secret six decades after Hiroshima and Nagasaki.)

In the second scenario, "Without such material from abroad, Iraq probably would not be able to make a weapon until 2007 to 2009, owing to inexperience in building and operating centrifuge facilities to produce highly enriched uranium and challenges in procuring the necessary equipment and expertise." Translation: Iraq could buy all the yellowcake or other forms of natural uranium in the world and still be five to seven years away from building a nuclear bomb. This timeline also assumes that Iraq's efforts to enrich this uranium and build a bomb would be uninterrupted by external or internal forces—whether UN inspectors, U.S. fighter jets, defections, revolts, etc.

So basically what the administration did was pull a switcheroo, using the timeline from Scenario A (months, not years) with the method from Scenario B (buying unenriched uranium and processing it domestically). Having accomplished this sleight of hand, the conclusion made more sense: We must kick out the inspectors and invade Iraq, ASAP, because Hussein is trying to get yellowcake and therefore could have a nuke any day.

While this was really nothing more than a frightening fiction created by conflating the two irreconcilable scenarios, it never got any attention in the media; the president's interpretation was based on classified documents. In any case, the distinction might have been too subtle for casual (or cynical) observers who could think parsing out the difference between months vs. years or enriched uranium vs. unenriched would be splitting hairs.

For intelligence analysts, however, getting the facts right is supposed to be their purpose. Or is this a naïve belief? In any case, the CIA's complicity in this prototypical Bush bait and switch tactic can be clearly seen when looking back at the annual reports the agency delivered to Congress on the global proliferation of weapons of mass destruction.

According to an article in *Newsday*, in the 1997 report Iraq only warranted three paragraphs, to the effect that Baghdad possessed dual-use equipment that could be used for biological or chemical programs. There was no mention of a nuclear weapons program. By 2002, however, the Iraq section was seven times as long, and warned that "all intelligence experts agree that Iraq is seeking nuclear weapons" and the country could produce a nuclear bomb "within a year" if it got its hands on weapons-grade material. The CIA also reported as late as 2001 that enforcement of the UN arms embargo on Iraq was "generally successful"—but this reference was dropped in the 2002 report sent to a White House that claimed the embargo wasn't working.

Donald Rumsfeld told Congress in July 2003 that no significant new evidence about Iraq's alleged weapons of mass destruction had been uncovered during the current administration. Why, then, had the reports become so shrill on the topic after Bush's inauguration, presenting the same intelligence with a completely different interpretation? After all, the CIA even had the same director under both Clinton and Bush.

Before the war, it could be argued that Clinton's White House had perhaps squelched damaging information about Iraq's WMD because they didn't want to make it an issue. After the war, however, this claim didn't hold water: Not only weren't any of the illegal weapons in question found, but the invading army didn't even seem particularly concerned to find them if they were there—even nuclear facilities were not adequately protected, with looters and locals suffering radiation poisoning before U.S. troops got around to securing them. Perhaps the generals were better at reading the intelligence than the White House.

"I'm afraid that the U.S. intelligence community, particularly the CIA . . . is sometimes quite sensitive to the political winds," Thielmann, formerly a senior intelligence official at the State Department, told *Newsday.* A CIA spokesman put it more delicately, noting that while the CIA had maintained its "integrity and objectivity," the agency "wants to be relevant to the policy process."

In any case, Bush's team wasn't going to leave it to chance, hoping the CIA would read their minds. Vice President Cheney, in particular, made a number of personal trips to the agency's headquarters in Langley, Virginia, to meet with low-level analysts who were reviewing the raw intelligence on Iraq. As one CIA official told the South African *Mail and Guardian,* "[He] sent signals, intended or otherwise, that a certain output was desired from here."

Other visitors to CIA headquarters representing the White House included Cheney's chief of staff, Scooter Libby, and ex–Speaker of the House Newt Gingrich, who joined the Pentagon as a "consultant" after 9/11. "That would freak people out," a former CIA official told the *New Republic.* "It is supposed to be an ivory tower. And that kind of pressure would be enormous on these young guys."

It is not known if these junior analysts were in fact intimidated enough by all this high-level attention or whether it affected the neutrality of their analysis. But for many, like ex–CIA agent Ray McGovern, who had himself at one time created NIE statements for presidents, this was all rather bizarre. "As though this were normal! . . . The visits were, in fact, unprecedented. During my 27-year career at the Central Intelligence Agency, no vice president ever came to us for a working visit."

McGovern was so irritated with the administration's treatment of the available intelligence that in January 2003, he cofounded Veteran

Intelligence Professionals for Sanity, "a group of 30 retired senior intelligence officers formed . . . to keep watch on the use/abuse of intelligence primarily regarding Iraq." The VIPS were mostly ex–CIA analysts, but also represented retired officers from the FBI, Defense Intelligence Agency, and other military and intelligence agencies who agreed that the Bush White House presented a unique danger for the integrity of U.S. intelligence and foreign policy.

"I think the administration is indeed pressuring the intelligence system, whether it be the CIA, FBI, or anyone else, to come up with the strongest possible evidence to indicate there is a genuine and immediate threat of attack by chemical, biological, or other weapons of mass destruction by terrorist groups and in particular those associated with Al Qaeda, and to link Iraq to that," said former CIA officer David MacMichael.

Even the Brookings Institute's Pollack, author of *The Threatening Storm: The Case for Invading Iraq,* was left wondering, after the war he had called for was underway, why it had been necessary to build the White House's campaign for invasion on a web of deception:

"Why was it necessary to put aside all of our other foreign policy priorities to go to war with Iraq in the spring of 2003?" Pollack wrote. "[D]istressingly, there seems to be more than a little truth to claims that some members of the administration skewed, exaggerated, and even distorted raw intelligence to coax the American people and reluctant allies into going to war against Iraq. . . . Needless to say, if the public felt Iraq was still several years away from acquiring a nuclear weapon rather than just a matter of months, there probably would have been much less support for war this spring."

The War Will Be a "Cakewalk"

"I believe demolishing Hussein's military power and liberating Iraq would be a cakewalk. Let me give simple, responsible reasons: (1) It was a cakewalk last time; (2) they've become much weaker; (3) we've become much stronger; and (4) now we're playing for keeps."

—Ken Adelman in the Washington Post on February 13, 2002— a full year before the first smart bomb fell on Baghdad.

THE FORMER ASSISTANT TO Donald Rumsfeld was just one of an orchestrated chorus of neoconservative voices in the media—later to be dubbed the "cakewalk brigade" by former *Newsweek* correspondent Arnaud de Borchgrave—who insisted that toppling Saddam would be both morally right and easy as pie. Appearing on PBS' *Wide Angle* later that year, then Defense Policy Board chairman Richard Perle described Saddam's regime as "a house of cards," poised to collapse at "the first whiff of gunpowder." The U.S. would just waltz its way into Baghdad, thanks to its awesome military technology and the support of grateful Iraqis, including Saddam's own troops. The rest—reconstruction, democracy, and even Middle East peace—would then just be a hop, skip, and jump away. And all this achieved at virtually no cost to either the U.S. troops or the average taxpayer.

As it turns out, the hawks were at least partly right—the military battle was, by most counts, a "cakewalk." But many observers soon began to use a very different word to describe its aftermath: *quagmire.*

As of this writing, seven months after the taking of Iraq, the United States finds itself in a war of attrition. The escalating violence, poor living conditions, and a steady succession of outgoing body bags is exacting a terrible toll on the soldiers who now find themselves enmeshed in a guerrilla war with invisible enemies.

"Some of the conditions I experienced over there were deplorable," said a female U.S. soldier, who had been deployed to Iraq along with her husband. He was still there when she wrote the letter to a nonprofit organization called Military Families Speak Out. "It sickens me every time I see news articles quoting dignitaries coming from there saying, 'The soldiers are in good spirits,' 'Morale is high.' I'm here to tell you, it's all lies. Morale is at an all-time low. Soldiers are hating life there, so much so, some are taking their own lives rather than deal with the situation. It has become that drastic."

The Republican Guard and other remnants of the Ba'athist regime did indeed "step aside," as Dick Cheney predicted on *Meet the Press,* but only to regroup as independent cells of resistance. Worse, groups with tribal and Islamic affiliations have reportedly joined their cause, united not in strategy or ideology but in their opposition to the U.S. presence.

In the opening weeks of the war, Richard Oakley, a former ambassador to Somalia and State Department counterterrorism coordinator, identified the Achilles' heel of U.S. foreign policy in a *Newsweek* online article: "We get carried away by our weapons, firepower, superiority, technology, all this kind of stuff, and we fail to look at the human factor. People will look for a chink in our armor, the same way David found a chink in Goliath's armor." On August 19, when a truck packed with 1,000 pounds of explosives detonated at UN headquarters and killed 22 people, that chink in the U.S. armor resembled a huge, gaping hole.

The situation is not likely to improve as popular anger at power outages, water shortages, rampant crime, and widespread unemployment continues to rise. The ham-handed plan for reconstruction is faltering in the face of widespread sabotage. Each terrorist attack evokes a fresh wave of anger at the U.S. for failing to provide basic security and services. In the aftermath of riots in the city of Basra—sparked by the lack of electricity—Karim Mnati, a clerk in the city's electricity department, told the *Los Angeles Times*, "It was just the beginning of the anger. It could get a lot worse. The people of Basra can tolerate this, but not for long. Maybe this is the start. And once it emanates from Basra, it will never stop."

The anger may well spread out from cities like Basra and Fallujah, all the way to Boise, Idaho, as the taxpayer is presented with a staggering Pentagon bill of some $150 billion and rising. The projected half-a-trillion deficit for 2004, the mounting U.S. casualties, political chaos in the Middle East, and serious setbacks in the battle against terrorism—each is likely to have a deep and lasting impact on the average American.

The brewing debacle in Iraq is not merely a result of errors in planning or poor decision-making. In devising their plan for Iraq, the Bush administration repeatedly and insistently dismissed the vast array of research assembled by think tanks and the warnings of its own officials in the State Department and the CIA. For a small group of men with little understanding of Iraq, warfare, or nation-building to believe that they alone knew better requires not just monumental arrogance but also a cavalier disregard for the consequences of being wrong.

Besides, whatever the Bush administration chose to believe before the war, the catastrophic results of its errors became quickly and painfully apparent in the immediate aftermath. Yet this president has not changed his course. Rather than admit error, he remains steadfast, unmoved by the deaths of Iraqis and his own soldiers, undaunted by the crippling costs to the American economy.

THE SEPTEMBER 11 ATTACKS marked a decisive turning point in U.S. foreign policy. Extraordinary measures were required for extraordinary times, argued the Bush administration in the months that followed. These included, it seems, not just waging the endless "war on terror," but also embracing an imperialist ideal long shunned by even the most die-hard militarists since the post–World War II era. "The American Empire: The Burden" was the title of Michael Ignatieff's controversial article in the *New York Times* magazine in January 2003, an apologia for the vision of a new world order defined by American supremacy. Michael Ledeen of the American Enterprise Institute best epitomized this new, open braggadocio when he said in *Harper's Magazine:* "Every 10 years or so, the United States needs to pick up some small crappy little country and throw it against the wall, just to show the world we mean business."

In order to preserve the United States' preeminent position as the world's lone superpower, the 1992 Defense Policy Guidelines draft, cowrit-ten by none other than Paul Wolfowitz and Scooter Libby, foresaw a world where U.S. military intervention would be "a constant fixture." A decade later, thanks to the newly ascendant fortune of Dick Cheney, a bulk of its recommendations became official U.S. foreign policy in September as part of the National Security Strategy document released by the Pentagon. Under the Bush doctrine, the United States would—in the words of foreign policy expert John Ikenberry—"use its unrivaled military power to man-age the global order." The central premise of this blueprint for global dom-ination is its equation of military strength with power. The United States military prowess would enable it to not just win a war, but to also shape entire nations and whole regions of the world.

TWO DAYS INTO THE war, U.S. General Tommy Franks bragged to the *Washington Post* about waging a brand new kind of war: "This will be a campaign unlike any other in history—a campaign characterized by shock, by surprise, by flexibility, by the employment of precise muni-tions on a scale never before seen, and by the application of overwhelm-ing force." "Smart" bombs, unmanned drones, and global intelligence-gathering systems were the basis for a revised defense strat-egy shaped by Defense Secretary Donald Rumsfeld and his protégés. The military campaign devised for Iraq would rely heavily on overwhelming airpower to keep down costs, the number of ground troops, and U.S. casualties, while carefully selecting key targets to "decapitate" Saddam's government, leaving the country's basic infrastructure intact. The aim was not just to "shock and awe" enemy troops into surrendering, but to also eliminate any thought or hope of resistance among the local population to ensure their compliance in the aftermath.

The brewing debacle in Iraq can be blamed as much on blind hubris as on the willful strategy of deception it inspired. The assumption was that this overwhelming military victory would pave the way for a quick and easy exit. According to the optimistic predictions of the Pentagon hawks in Undersecretary of Defense for Policy Douglas Feith's office, once the top Ba'ath party echelons were eliminated, the bulk of the Iraqi military, police, and bureaucracy would join the U.S. to undertake the main responsibility of securing order in the country. With basic services in place, the U.S. would quickly begin the task of rebuilding the nation and earn the long-lasting gratitude of an already welcoming Iraqi people. The administration could then hand off the onerous task of governing to its carefully appointed Iraqi regime and withdraw its troops within a matter of months.

When General Eric Shinseki, the Army chief of staff, told reporters a month before the war that "something of the order of several hundred thousand soldiers" would be required to stabilize postwar Iraq, Deputy Defense Secretary Paul Wolfowitz knocked him down for being "wildly off the mark." As reported in the *Financial Times,* Wolfowitz said, "I am reasonably certain that [the Iraqis] will greet us as liberators; and that will help us to keep requirements down." Dick Cheney would reiterate the message weeks later on NBC's *Meet the Press*: "[T]o suggest that we need several hundred thousand troops there after military operations cease, after the conflict ends, I don't think is accurate. I think that's an overstatement." The wrong-headed unilateralism during the lead-up to the war was based almost entirely on this illusionary scenario. Why share power to spread the burden when the U.S. could get the lion's share of the postwar booty, credit, and influence at little cost to itself?

Tim Carney, a former diplomat recruited to serve the U.S.-led administration in Iraq, told the *Washington Post* in July, "Everyone thought it could be done on a small investment and that Iraqis could be mobilized to do the bulk of the job." The Bush administration repeatedly assured Congress that the resources required for a military battle would suffice for reconstruction. On July 27, 2003, Paul Wolfowitz told *Meet the Press'* Tim Russert, "It's hard to conceive that it would take more forces to provide stability in post-Saddam Iraq than it would take to conduct the war itself and to secure the surrender of Saddam's security forces and his army. Hard to imagine." It was hard to imagine, even though the CIA had warned the White House in February 2003 that armed opposition was inevitable after the war.

In the summer of 2002, the State Department created the Future of Iraq Project, which brought together Iraqi exiles from around the world and a team of international experts to put together a comprehensive plan for the reconstruction of Iraq—only to have their recommendations ignored by the Pentagon. A State Department official told the *Financial Times,* "The short and brutal [story] is that we did almost a year's worth of planning, extensive efforts, external and internal, combined it, put it in a package, offered it to OSD [Office of the Secretary of Defense] and they refused it." The most telling indictment of the Pentagon's arrogance was delivered in late July by retired Lieutenant Colonel Karen Kwiatkowski, who worked in Feith's office from May 2002 through February 2003. Describing the "functional isolation" of the Pentagon team, she told NPR in August 2003, "If you mentioned in a staff meeting, if you mentioned to your superiors, 'Well, State has indicated they have some concerns here . . .'—these kinds of things were met with, 'It doesn't matter. We're not bending. Don't listen to those people. They don't know what they're doing, and they're not on board.'"

The men in charge of the Iraq policy, be it Feith, Cheney, Wolfowitz, or Rumsfeld, instead chose to rely exclusively on the upbeat picture painted by Ahmed Chalabi and the Iraqi National Congress—the same people that retired General Anthony Zinni, the former head of Central Command for U.S. forces in the Middle East, once ridiculed as "silk-suited, Rolex-wearing guys in London." When asked by Tim Russert, just days before the war, whether Americans are prepared for a "long, costly, and bloody battle," Dick Cheney cited a leading member of the INC in his response: "I've talked with a lot of Iraqis in the last several months myself, had them to the White House . . . like Kanan Makiya who's a professor at Brandeis, but an Iraqi, he's written great books about the subject, knows the country intimately, and is a part of the democratic opposition and resistance. The read we get on the people of Iraq is there is no question but what they want is to get rid of Saddam Hussein and they will welcome as liberators the United States when we come to do that." Within a month after the war, it was clear that the White House should have paid better attention to the likes of General Zinni—the man who predicted last August that supporting the INC could turn an Iraq war into "the Bay of Goats."

The easy optimism of the likes of Rumsfeld and Wolfowitz was left mostly unchallenged in the media in the months leading up to the war. The debate instead centered almost exclusively on military merits of an Iraq war, thanks to the White House strategy of lowering expectations to declare "success"; the media's infatuation with the drama of combat; and the antiwar advocates who mistakenly chose to emphasize the risks of a long-drawn, bloody battle, an argument that was well-suited to Bush's interests. Dire predictions of a Stalingrad-style battle for Baghdad and high estimates for U.S. casualties dominated TV talk shows, while the Bush administration's other, more important claims about the likely fallout of such a victory received little or no scrutiny. War was clearly sexier than reconstruction. The only important question dominating media coverage was whether the U.S. would win the confrontation with Saddam's army—a question that soon proved irrelevant to any meaningful definition of "victory."

This narrow conception of victory was not surprising in a nation that had grown accustomed to "quickie" wars. Whether in the first Gulf War, Panama, or even the relatively disastrous stint in Somalia, Americans were familiar with a "bomb 'em and leave 'em" style of warfare. In telegenic military engagements like the Gulf War and Afghanistan, more soldiers died moving equipment than in combat. These wars decisively established the awesome might of U.S. firepower—Adelman referred repeatedly to these previous wars to bolster his "cakewalk" thesis, pointing out with undisguised pride that "our gizmos worked wonders" in the Gulf War and later against the Taliban.

As it turns out, Afghanistan, where President Bush made similar promises to restore the nation and foster democracy, did indeed provide an instructive parallel. The fallout from the Afghan War illustrated a simple fact: "Gizmos" can win a war but not the hearts and minds of a people. Less than a year after a rousing military victory, the U.S. troops were no longer in control of major parts of the countryside and the Taliban were already regrouping and regaining their strength. At the time, however, the media with its short attention span was far too absorbed in Iraq to pay much attention to the unraveling situation in Afghanistan. The first post-9/11 war was still seen as an immense success—fueling the dangerous notion that the United States could simply walk into nations and remake them in its own image.

Moreover, the post-9/11 climate was more conducive to asserting the invincibility of American power than pointing to our vulnerabilities. While some in the mainstream media were beginning to speak of the "chilling effect" on dissent in the late summer of 2002, the domestic debate over Iraq remained muted. Apart from a few exceptions such as Senator Robert Byrd and Representative Dennis Kucinich, Democrats were cowed into silence, afraid to have their "patriotism" questioned in a mid-election year. As the polls in the latter part of 2002 show, the majority of the American public chose to rally around the president despite reservations about the wisdom of unilateral action. The idea that the United States could take on the "bad guys" with ease and at little cost was deeply comforting. Bill Clinton summed up the national mood when he explained the Democratic electoral rout in the fall of 2002: "When people feel uncertain, they'd rather have somebody who's strong and wrong than somebody who's weak and right."

Richard Goldstein, executive editor of the *Village Voice*, described this phenomenon as the rise of the "Neo-macho Man." In the wake of 9/11, argued Goldstein, "the once-mocked figure of the dominant male has become a real-life hero. Saluting the new spirit of patriarchal vitality. *People* included Rumsfeld in its most recent list of the sexiest men alive. In his feckless swagger, we see the timeless union of militarism and macho." No one was better positioned to take advantage of this culture of hyper-masculinity than Republican hawks with their kick-some-ass attitude.

THE WAR, WHEN IT came, merely confirmed this delusion of omnipotence. There were some sticky moments in the early weeks, when the Rumsfeld doctrine seemed to run into trouble. Contrary to the White House's predictions, Iraqis did not seem particularly eager to either join arms with the U.S. forces or welcome them with garlands, and the Fedayeen put up more of a fight than expected. But for the most part, the military battle was a "cakewalk," at least for the United States. The victory that followed also provided the two most powerful images of the administration's bright and shining lie: the toppling of Saddam Hussein's statue and George Bush's victory speech aboard the USS Lincoln. Both these "symbolic" moments fed the dangerous illusion that the war was over—that might had indeed made everything all right.

On April 9, the Bush administration scored its first major photo-op in the second Gulf War, when the international media watched a couple hundred Iraqis bring down a massive statue of Saddam Hussein in Baghdad's Firdos Square. That Iraqis needed the assistance of an American tank recovery vehicle to bring the statue down was just the perfect touch that completed the symbolism: The U.S. military had liberated the Iraqi people from the tyranny of Saddam. "Saddam Hussein is now taking his rightful place alongside Hitler, Stalin, Lenin, and Ceausescu in the pantheon of failed, brutal dictators," Rumsfeld told reporters at a Pentagon briefing in Washington.

As expected, images of the the toppled statue were replayed over and over again on televisions across the country, accompanied by words such as "breathtaking," "historic," and "liberation." William Safire wrote in the *New York Times* the next day, "[L]ike newly freed Russians pulling down the statue of the hated secret police chief in Dzerzhinsky Square, the newly freed Iraqis toppled the figure of their tyrant and ground their shoes into the face of Saddam Hussein." The small number of Iraqis involved, the misleading perspective of the close-up shots, and the presence of INC supporters—issues first raised by the independent media— would rob the moment of its glory in the weeks that followed. Also downplayed at the time was a more telling and spontaneous moment in this public relations exercise when a young marine briefly draped a U.S. flag over Saddam's head, a gesture that upset both the watching Arab world and folks in the Pentagon briefing room. And when several marines were killed in a suicide bombing near Firdos Square two days later, few other than *Independent* columnist Robert Fisk seemed to note the ironic significance of the event.

Within weeks, the U.S. cakewalk began melting in the 120-degree oven of Iraqi anger. The images of celebration were quickly replaced by those of looting, as roving bands of marauders indiscriminately pillaged hospitals, museums, embassies, and government buildings. The anarchy that characterized the month of April was an early sign of the fundamental errors in the administration's postwar plan, and more important, its flawed sense of priorities. But happily for the administration, the American public appeared only momentarily stunned by the events in Iraq, thanks mainly to big media. MSNBC correspondent Ashleigh Banfield in an uncharacteristically candid speech to students at Kansas State University said, "I am not so sure that we in America are hesitant to do this again, to fight another war, because it looked like a glorious and courageous and so successful, terrific endeavor." According to a PIPA (Program on International Policy Attitudes) poll released April 29, an overwhelming 75 percent of all Americans supported Bush's Iraq policy. It was an ideal moment for George Bush's first campaign appearance in the guise of a "victory" speech.

On May 1, the president landed on the USS Abraham Lincoln on a Navy plane, strutting across the aircraft carrier in a scene stolen straight out of a Hollywood blockbuster (*Top Gun*, to be specific). The setting, the fighter pilot uniform, and his cocky demeanor were intended to convey the immense power of the American war-making machine. The military victory had already been cause for undisguised gloating among the neoconservatives, who saw in it the confirmation of the United States' unassailable supremacy. In an article titled "The Restoration of American Awe" in the conservative *Weekly Standard*, Reuel Marc Gerecht of the American Enterprise Institute wrote, "The virtually nonexistent Battle of Baghdad decisively accomplished what the first several days of the war—the 'shock-and-awe' portion—had not . . . America's armed forces had taken from Saddam Hussein his *hayba*—the awe that belongs to indomitable authority."

Bush's own speech, backed by a "Mission Accomplished" banner, echoed this self-satisfied infatuation with American power:

"Operation Iraqi Freedom was carried out with a combination of precision and speed and boldness the enemy did not expect, and the world had not seen before. From distant bases or ships at sea, we sent planes and missiles that could destroy an enemy division, or strike a single bunker. Marines and soldiers charged to Baghdad across 350 miles of hostile ground, in one of the swiftest advances of heavy arms in history. You have shown the world the skill and the might of the American Armed Forces."

In the words of Michael Ledeen, the U.S. had just taken Iraq and thrown it against the wall to show the world it meant business. It felt so good that the hawks in the administration were chomping at the bit for their next piece of "action." Rumsfeld and company were already issuing threatening statements aimed variously at Iran, Syria, and North Korea. Vividly apparent in Bush's victory performance was the pervasive aggressiveness that has characterized his administration's foreign policy.

THE DREADED Q-WORD, "quagmire," had already entered the media vocabulary in late June—though carefully restricted to the inside pages of the major newspapers. Less than two months after George Bush's triumphant speech, leading commentators were beginning to describe Iraq as a nation spiraling out of control. Contrary to the rhetoric emanating from the White House, the promised "liberation" had all the warning signs of a long, bloody occupation almost from day one—an enraged local population; severe religious and tribal divisions; nervous troops quick to fire and often unable to differentiate friend from foe; and the nascent signs of nationalist resistance. None of which were mentioned, let alone accounted for, in the administration's plan for reconstructing Iraq.

The entire plan to invade and occupy Iraq conceived within the Pentagon was one extended rosy scenario. An unnamed administration official told the *Financial Times* that the network of hawks led by the Pentagon's Douglas Feith "all along felt that this was going to be not just a cakewalk, it was going to be 60–90 days, a flip-over and handoff, a lateral or whatever to [Ahmed] Chalabi and the INC. The DOD could then wash its hands of the whole affair and depart quickly, smoothly, and swiftly. And there would be a democratic Iraq that was amenable to our wishes and desires left in its wake. And that's all there was to it." Better yet, it was all going to pay for itself thanks to the bountiful supplies of Iraqi oil. Events in Iraq would soon prove the reality to be far different and the plan to be nothing less than surreal.

Come September, the official cost of the war and its aftermath was a billion dollars a week, borne almost entirely by the American taxpayer.

The Pentagon had reneged on its promise to cut down on troop strength from 140,000 to 30,000 by September, earning the ire of soldiers and their families. The same go-it-alone administration that questioned the "relevance" of the United Nations was scrambling to persuade the Security Council to help the overstretched and exhausted U.S. military keep the peace. The reconstruction effort, already hampered by the myopic assumptions of its planners, was reeling from a series of well-aimed bombings of oil and water pipelines. And much of whatever goodwill the United States had earned by ousting their tyrant had clearly been lost over months of occupation, characterized by unemployment, crime, shortages, and deaths of Iraqi civilians caught in the crossfire of a guerrilla war—a war that threatened to spin out of control with the entry of Islamic jihadis eager to take on a U.S. army stranded in a hostile nation.

According to a CNN report on August 26, the number of U.S. soldiers who died in Iraq since May 1, the date of George Bush's triumphant speech, stood at 139—officially higher than the toll of the military battle. It marked the decisive moment when the American public finally recognized that their nation was once again embroiled in a dead-end war, with no hope of an early exit.

Nearly a month later, on September 24, the total death toll since the start of hostilities on March 20, 2003 had climbed to 341, the wounded to somewhere between 1,600 and 10,000, depending on who in the military is doing the counting and what type of injuries are counted. The casualty rate in Iraq at the time of this book's publication in early October 2003 was three to six deaths and 40 wounded every week, according to U.S. Army Lieutenant General Ricardo Sanchez.

HAWKS, BOTH WITHIN AND outside of the administration, repeatedly conjured up images of delirious Iraqis welcoming the invading U.S. soldiers with open arms. In March 2003, Paul Wolfowitz ebulliently declared, "Like the people of France in the 1940s, they view us as their hoped-for liberator." When the scenes of joyous celebration remained muted during the war, his neoconservative allies outside the administration remained unfazed. Danielle Pletka, vice president of the American Enterprise Institute, sweepingly declared to the *Guardian*, "The neoconservative analysis is shared by every Iraqi I know. There's a regrettable tendency on the part of reporters and pundits to act like children in the back of the car, and scream at every moment, 'Are we there yet?'" Her statement reflected what Tom Carothers, analyst for the Carnegie Endowment for International Peace, described in the same article as "the neoconservative fallback position—'that even if there are people who aren't certain of our intention, we'll show them over time.'" If the Iraqis did not embrace their American "liberators" today, they would do so tomorrow, the month after, or in six months.

Time, unfortunately, has not been the administration's ally.

At the core of the difficulties faced by the Paul Bremer–led administration in Iraq is a cockeyed agenda that prioritizes the flawed assumptions of the rulers at the expense of the Iraqi people. This ham-handed approach—characterized by a combination of arrogance, callousness, and outright stupidity—was made painfully apparent within the first few weeks of looting after the war. By posting troops solely around the oil and interior ministries (central to this supposedly self-financing war) and standing by while looters pillaged through shops, hospitals, and priceless artifacts at the museum, the Pentagon sent a clear message about its priorities. "The Americans are only here to occupy us and drive us into ruin," a hapless store owner told London's *Sunday Telegraph*, expressing the collective fears of a people who had already endured the Iran-Iraq war, the first Gulf War, and years of crippling sanctions imposed and overseen by the United Nations. Those fears were not dispelled by Rumsfeld's own reaction to the looting. "Freedom is untidy," he scolded reporters. "Stuff happens."

The "untidy" situation in Iraq has shown few signs of improving. Electricity and gasoline are in short supply in a nation swimming in oil—so much so that Iraq is now importing essential refined oil products, including petrol, diesel, and cooking gas. Murder, robbery, kidnapping, rape, and carjackings have become the norm in a nation marked by scarcity and a 50 percent unemployment rate. In July, according to the *Guardian*, Baghdad's mortuary handled 47 times as many gunshot deaths as in the same period in 2002. Without electricity to power the pumps, the water supply is erratic and mostly unsafe. Two wars, 12 years of sanctions, and postwar looting and sabotage have left water processing plants in poor shape. In Basra, the malfunctioning sewage plants are polluting the canals used by locals for drinking and bathing, creating a serious risk of cholera. To date, basic resources remain scarce even in Umm Qasr, the first city captured by the coalition forces. Kadem Muhsin, 30, a former driver who can't afford the gasoline he needs to work, told the *Boston Globe*, "We are like dead people. Before the war, we had electricity, we had water. Only the Ba'athist party bothered us. But those are small troubles if you compare it with now."

Popular anger at the abysmal conditions, made more unbearable by the unremitting 120-degree heat, was directed unequivocally at the United States. In British-controlled Basra, long considered the most peaceful city in postwar Iraq, the rage at the coalition forces escalated into bloody rioting and took four days to quell. Plagued by gasoline shortages, power blackouts, and constant gun battles, Iraqis lashed out at the powerful army which used its vast resources to wreak devastation on their land but now seemed unwilling or unable to fix the damage. A resident of Basra told the *Los Angeles Times*, "All of us are very angry at the coalition. When the coalition came, we were happy and welcomed them, but they did nothing. On the contrary, they made more of a crisis. They are superpowers, they can do anything they want." In the aftermath of the bombing of the UN headquarters, the residents of Baghdad were angry at the terrorists, but reserved the greater part of their wrath for the United States. Layla Yahyag, who lost her brother in the attack, told *USA Today*, "We want Saddam again. We don't want American soldiers. There is no security. They promised us help."

Over the past months, the administration has been stubbornly unwilling to address or even acknowledge the real reasons for its failure to win the goodwill of the Iraqis. On April 30, at a time when much of the country was reeling from lack of electricity, drinking water, and crime, Donald Rumsfeld broadcast his first speech to the Iraqi people. "Coalition forces are working in close partnership with Iraqi citizens to restore order and basic services," he declared. "Each day that goes by, conditions in Iraq are improving. In fact, in a number of parts of the country, people already have more food, more medicine, more water, more electricity than they had under the old regime." Sadly, lacking the electricity to power their radios or televisions, few Iraqis heard his stirring speech. It was a fitting moment of irony that revealed the yawning gulf between a willfully blind administration and the grim reality on the ground.

The very same day, Rumsfeld also addressed the U.S. troops stationed in Iraq. "You came not to conquer, not to occupy, but to liberate, and the Iraqi people know this," he said. This fine distinction was lost on the residents of Fallujah, where U.S. soldiers had killed 13 people during a pro-Saddam march just a few days before. While the U.S. military claimed that they were merely returning fire—a charge Iraqis on the scene strenuously denied—the shootings were seen as yet another example of American brutality. Fallujah was just one of many such incidents where Iraqi civilians died at the hands of increasingly nervous soldiers, who found themselves embroiled in a guerrilla war. In July, an abortive raid to capture Saddam Hussein resulted in the death of 11 Iraqi civilians, when U.S. troops started shooting indiscriminately at motorists who approached a barbed wire fence that the soldiers had placed without warning across the road. An eyewitness told the *Independent*'s Robert Fisk, "The Americans didn't try to help the civilians they had shot, not once. They let the car burn and left the bodies where they lay, even the children. It was we who had to take them to the hospitals."

An Amnesty International report issued in July accused U.S. forces of using tactics that are a "strong echo" of Saddam's modus operandi.

According to the organization, apart from the shoot-to-kill incidents, U.S. soldiers routinely snatch people off the street and put them in prison, where they are subjected to torture and denied access to relatives or lawyers. While the Pentagon has refused to keep track of the number of Iraqi civilian casualties, the nonprofit organization IraqBodyCount.net, run by a team of American and British academics, puts the latest number at roughly 8,000. And that number does not include the many who die indirectly from the violence and chaos created by the invasion, be it from flying shrapnel or violent crime. It does not include the many who are injured and rushed to dilapidated hospitals, where the walls are streaked with blood and vomit and basic equipment is still in short supply. For Iraqis, each passing day adds to the heavy human toll of their "liberation."

The truth is that the Bush administration has not yet made a good faith effort to serve the welfare of the Iraqi people. It instead has chosen to pursue its own lopsided agenda—mainly the elimination of the "most wanted" members of Saddam's regime—and used rhetoric to mask its many failures. In August, the Bremer administration released a 24-page report titled "Results in Iraq: 100 Days Toward Security and Freedom," detailing its "successes." In this fictional Iraq, electricity "is now more equitably distributed," water supplies are "at pre-conflict levels," and "healthcare, previously available only for Ba'athist elite, is now available to all Iraqis." On October 9, despite increasing chaos, President Bush in a New Hampshire speech said the situation in Iraq was "a lot better than you probably think." While such lies may temporarily lull the American public, they are unlikely to win over Iraqis who have to live the uncomfortable reality that the president would prefer to deny.

Denial is never a sound long-term strategy, not even for an administration that has honed it to an art form. Returning from a visit to Iraq in late August, Senator John McCain warned the White House, "Time is not on our side. People in 125-degree heat, with no electricity and no fuel, are going to become angry in a big hurry." Mohammed Jaff, a 28-

year-old building contractor, couldn't agree more. "The Americans know the Iraqis will not tolerate this more than two or three months," he told the *Los Angeles Times.* "I could very easily take my machine gun and kill two or three Americans each day, but not yet."

ON AUGUST 26, 2002, Dick Cheney told the Veterans of Foreign Wars, "Regime change in Iraq would bring about a number of benefits to the region. . . . Extremists in the region would have to rethink their strategy of jihad. Moderates throughout the region would take heart. And our ability to advance the Israeli-Palestinian peace process would be enhanced, just as it was following the liberation of Kuwait in 1991." It pretty much summed up the Bush administration's Iraq plan.

Almost exactly a year later, on August 21, 2003, Rumsfeld was standing next to General John Abizaid, chief of U.S. Central Command, as he told reporters that terrorism was the "number one security threat" in Iraq. In the wake of the UN bombing, Paul Bremer and other Bush officials eagerly claimed that "hundreds" of jihadis were crossing the border into Iraq, ready to take on the United States in a holy war. It marked a sudden shift of focus for an administration that had insisted for months that the escalating violence in Iraq was being orchestrated by remnants of the Ba'athist regime—or "dead-enders" as Rumsfeld liked to call them. But it was hardly the first time that Bush officials would change their tune to fit shifting circumstances.

In the lead-up to the war, the administration hawks assumed that Saddam's army would simply surrender at first sight of the advancing U.S. army. Richard Perle declared in the summer of 2002, "Of the 400,000 in Saddam's army, I'll be surprised if 10 percent are loyal to Saddam. And the other 90 percent won't be completely passive. Many of them will come over to the opposition." According to a *Boston Globe* article, when CIA officials warned Rumsfeld, Cheney, and the president in a formal briefing in February of the probability of a guerrilla war— "A quick military victory in Iraq will likely be followed by armed resistance from remnants of the Ba'ath party and Fedayeen Saddam irregulars"—they were simply ignored. However, as the weeks of sporadic but persistent postwar violence turned into months, the White House adopted a new mantra—pockets of evil Ba'athist loyalists were undermining the future of Iraq—to explain away all their difficulties.

The bloodshed in Fallujah was blamed on Saddam fanatics seeking to draw U.S. forces into shooting civilians, as were the increasing number of grenade and machine-gun attacks that followed. In July, when Al Qaeda claimed responsibility for the wave of attacks, Rumsfeld ironically dismissed the claim on NBC's *Meet the Press*: "We're still in a war. There's still a lot of people from the Ba'athists and Fedayeen, Saddam-regime types who are there, who are disadvantaged by the fact that their regime has been thrown out, and would like to get back." The "war on terror" angle would have to wait a couple more months to gain currency with the administration. The focus on Saddam defined the Pentagon's strategy in postwar Iraq. The U.S. military spent most of the first few months investing immense resources in Operation Sidewinder, which was aimed at tracking down and eliminating the "most wanted" members of the deposed regime. Each capture or killing in turn provided fodder for a vast public relations spectacle, aimed at convincing the public that the U.S. was in control of a nation in turmoil.

When Saddam's sons, Uday and Qusay, were killed on July 22, the Pentagon released the pictures of their bloodied corpses to ensure a media spectacle. Rumsfeld called it "absolutely the correct decision," and told reporters: "The Iraqi people have been waiting for confirmation of that and they, in my view, they deserved that confirmation." The focus on the Ba'athists allowed the White House to ignore the growing anti-American sentiment among Iraqis, and to pretend that their lack of cooperation was driven by their fear of Saddam rather than their hostility toward the U.S. presence. At the time, even U.S. commanders on the ground were becoming skeptical of the loyalist conspiracy conjured up by the administration. Lieutenant Colonel Eric Wesley, of the Army's 3rd

Infantry Division in Fallujah, told the *San Francisco Chronicle* in early July, "I think it's a bit of everything—Fedayeen, ex-military, and unemployed workers sitting around fuming in the heat. From what we've seen around here, it's probably small, disconnected groups, which will be difficult to root out." Iraqis interviewed in the same article were more blunt: "It's mostly young people, who have no jobs, and they see the Americans committing abuses and occupying the country, so they have no choice but to fight. It is a national struggle and an Islamic struggle." Not surprisingly, 11 U.S. soldiers died in the week following the killing of Saddam's sons, giving lie to the administration's claims.

The Bush administration appears singularly incapable of acknowledging the reality of Iraqi nationalism—as though the concept that Iraqis can oppose both Saddam and the U.S. is too fantastic to comprehend. Making his rounds of the Sunday talk shows the weekend after the UN bombing in August, Bremer vehemently denied any possibility of an Iraqi resistance on *This Week with George Stephanopoulos:* "Well, let me first object to the word 'resistance.' The people who are resisting here are resisting the vision of a democratic and free Iraq, they're not resisting us." In order to recognize the reality of the guerrilla war, Bremer and other Bush officials will first have to accept that their entire adventure in imperialism was based on a false premise—that the simple act of eliminating Saddam's regime would reconcile Iraqis, armed or otherwise, to U.S. occupation. E. J. Dionne wrote in the *Washington Post,* "It's astonishing that Bush and his advisers never seemed to take seriously the obvious possibility: that many, perhaps most, Iraqis—especially the Shiite Muslim majority so oppressed by Saddam Hussein—could be perfectly happy to have the United States get rid of their dictator and then want U.S. troops to leave immediately."

It is this tone-deaf obstinacy that has doomed the Bush plan from the very beginning—even before the war began. Despite being briefed repeatedly by a wide array of experts—at the Council on Foreign Relations (overseen by a Republican former defense secretary and member of the Defense Policy Board, James Schlesinger), the Atlantic

Council, the Center for Strategic and International Studies, and the United States Institute of Peace—the Pentagon simply refused to believe it would need to use its troops for peacekeeping. The three main prongs of the Bush strategy—a relatively small number of troops, strategic bombing, and unilateral force—relied on this deluded assumption that flew in the face of the facts.

Returning from a trip to Iraq in July, Paul Wolfowitz in a moment of relative candor admitted that the postwar plans had indeed gone awry. He told reporters, "No army units, at least none of any significant size, came over to our side so that we could use them as Iraqi forces with us today. Second, the police turned out to require a massive overhaul. Third, and worst of all, it was difficult to imagine before the war that the criminal gang of sadists and gangsters who have run Iraq for 35 years would continue fighting." In other words, the entire reconstruction effort went into a tailspin within the first few weeks of April.

To begin with, the widespread looting effectively undermined the main benefit of precision bombing. The administration had meticulously planned its air campaign in order to leave key government facilities, cultural sites, hospitals, and other civilian buildings intact—ready to use after the war. But with a military unprepared to maintain basic law and order, most of these facilities were soon ransacked and destroyed. Major General Buford Blount, commander of the Army's 3rd Infantry Division, told *USA Today*, "Looting wasn't taken into military consideration. It never came in the order process that it would be a major problem." The devastation, however, irretrievably destroyed any hopes of a quick recovery. Jay Garner, who was in charge of Iraqi reconstruction at the time, admitted, "Our plan was to immediately stand up 20 of 23 existing ministries. But 17 of them had been vaporized." The effort to reinstate members of the Ba'ath police in Baghdad in response to the looting created widespread outrage among residents, forcing U.S. officials to back down.

Even as the U.S. military wrestled with a chaotic Baghdad, Islamic fundamentalists rapidly moved in to fill the power vacuum in the Shia-dominated countryside. Having ignored the warnings of the State Department, the Pentagon now found itself facing the unexpected threat of religious nationalism—a prospect that its friends in the exile-dominated INC had downplayed. By the end of April, religious organizations in cities like Kut and Karbala had created de facto local governments and were talking about throwing the U.S. out. A resident of Kut told the *Independent,* "The Americans did nothing after the Ba'ath fled, so the religious leaders have started to run things. We are following what the Koran has taught us. We do not need foreigners to tell us what to do."

There was little a force of 150,000 soldiers spread over a country the size of Iraq could do to forestall the domino effect of the initial weeks of chaos. A 1999 war exercise, supervised by Anthony Zinni as commander of U.S. forces in Iraq, recommended a force of 400,000 troops to invade and stabilize Iraq. According to an article in *USA Today* by Barbara Slavin and Dave Moniz, a National Security Council memo outlining the lessons of recent peacekeeping operations prepared in February put the required troop strength at 500,000. But Rumsfeld, driven by his ideological commitment to a small ground force, firmly rejected any such suggestion. Thomas White, who served as secretary of the Army until Rumsfeld pushed him out after the war, said that any suggestion of a larger ground force "was not music anyone down the hallway [in Rumsfeld's office] wanted to listen to."

By the end of the month, it was clear that there would be no quick handoff, but instead the U.S. forces were facing a long war of attrition. Yet in early May, the administration also eliminated a valuable source of assistance. The Iraqi army was demobilized on the recommendation of Paul Bremer—a decision that alienated the Iraqi troops and at the same time helped spread weapons all over Iraq. According to former Iraqi Army Brigadier General Mohammad Abdullah Nour, "The munitions were everywhere, even on the sidewalks. Not just 500-pound bombs, but 2-ton or 5-ton bombs or 10-ton bombs. The Iraqi army was scattered all over Iraq, and when they abandoned their posts, they left the weapons there." Unsurprisingly, these weapons ended up in the hands of various resistance groups, including, experts say, the people who blew up the UN headquarters in Baghdad using a bomb made of Soviet-era munitions, the mainstay of Saddam's military.

The task of peacekeeping now fell almost entirely on the shoulders of U.S. soldiers ill-equipped to do the job. The same experts who briefed the Pentagon on the need for a police force also advised against using troops whose training included only "shoot to kill and retreat." Their assessment was confirmed in July by John J. Hamre, who as president of the Center for Strategic and International Studies completed a report for the Pentagon on postwar challenges: "The reaction over there from folks closer to the ground was that they were not given very good preparation for what they encountered." In Wolfowitz's own words, the U.S. troops are trained to use "actionable intelligence and pursue killers," not manage the delicate task of peacekeeping.

The psychological toll of executing an increasingly impossible mission soon began to show. Lori, an unhappy 21-year-old private, told *Newsweek*: "I feel like I've died and gone to hell. . . . On my good days, I feel like maybe we're at least doing something worthwhile for these people. There aren't many good days. On my bad days, I feel like getting my machine gun and opening up on every one of them." As U.S. casualties continued to mount, individual soldiers reportedly beat, robbed, and even killed civilians. The troops had become bogged down in what Israeli analyst Ze'ev Schiff described as the triangle of occupation: "The coalition forces are now in the middle of the inevitable triangle—one side is the humanitarian aid, including distributing food and water to the civilian population, another side is suicide bombings against coalition forces, and the third side is jumpy, trigger-happy soldiers at checkpoints." The result is a yawning divide between the rulers and ruled that has now become almost impossible to bridge.

In fact, the Pentagon had already sown the seeds of a guerrilla resistance within the first month after the war, miring its own soldiers in a war for which they were poorly equipped. Simply put, the administration's Iraq plan was dead on arrival.

IN 1963, MARTIN LUTHER KING JR. wrote, "Our scientific power has outrun our spiritual power. We have guided missiles and misguided men." The unassailable belief in military supremacy has defined the Bush administration's foreign policy. Its dream of global domination powered by a unilateral, aggressive military policy requires the fatal belief that wars can be won at little cost to the victor.

Rumsfeld's strategy assumed that a force of 160,000 troops could rely on its immense firepower to awe an entire nation into submission. There would be no need to seek the help of others or the consent of the rest of the world. It would also keep costs down. In Douglas Feith's words, the decision to limit the number of troops was "strategic and goes far beyond Iraq. This is part of his [Rumsfeld's] thinking about defense transformation. It's an old way of thinking to say that the United States should not do anything without hundreds of thousands of troops. That makes our military less usable." Inexpensive military engagements were central to a foreign policy that planned to rely on direct confrontation to achieve its goals.

It was on the strength of this misplaced conviction that the United States repeatedly ruled out any involvement of the UN and European nations in the immediate aftermath. When the United Nations offered to step in to help in April, arguing that an international force of seasoned peacekeepers would help secure the nation to speed up reconstruction, the Bush White House spurned the offer. Even though the country was still in chaos in May, the Pentagon announced that it expected to cut troop strength down to 30,000 by September. Rumsfeld kept to his optimistic predictions on troop strength until mid-July, when he abruptly switched course and announced that the troops could expect to stay at least another year, perhaps even "indefinitely." The reaction of the soldiers on an ABC News report was shockingly raw. "I've got my own 'Most Wanted' list," said a sergeant, "The aces in my deck are Paul Bremer, Donald Rumsfeld, George Bush, and Paul Wolfowitz."

As part of his farewell speech in June, General Shinseki, prophetic as ever, warned his colleagues: "Beware the 12-division strategy for a 10-division army." It is a reality that this administration refuses to accept, even though the perils of ignoring it are clear. In the wake of the UN headquarters bombing, Rumsfeld continues to insist that there is little or no need to increase the number of U.S. troops on the ground, even though Paul Bremer has admitted that they are "stretched thin" across Iraq. Experts like James Dobbins, the former special envoy to Afghanistan, now say that more than 300,000 troops will be needed to bring the country back under control—reiterating the prewar estimates of the NSC. But this administration is unwilling to make the compromises needed to bring in the foreign troops it so desperately requires. When Secretary of State Colin Powell went to the UN to ask the Security Council to mandate an international force, he made it clear that the U.S. was willing to share the burden of peacekeeping but not the authority.

The Bush administration continues to stand firm but our own soldiers are paying a high price. According to a *Washington Post* analysis, there have been few pauses in the steadily increasing tally, apart from a brief 12-day lull in May. More important, since May 1, the army has suffered nearly all the deaths from hostile action. According to the *New York Times*, the death toll since the end of major combat operations at the time of writing this book is 183. Both Democrats and Republicans have urged the White House to "put more boots on the ground" to ease the strain, as have military families. The White House's response has thus far been limited to pat phrases lauding the "sacrifice" of the dead. Many soldiers themselves are simply exhausted, homesick, and disillusioned both with their generals who sold them the shining lie of a quick war of liberation and the nation that seems unwilling to be rescued. Private First Class Eric Rattler told ABC News, "I used to want to help these people, but now I don't really care about them anymore." Contrary to what the U.S. soldiers were told, the road to Baghdad did not lead them home but straight into the limbo of a dead-end war.

It isn't surprising that the Bush administration has little or no interest in the welfare of its own men and women in uniform. After all, this is the White House that tried to cut the allowances of the soldiers stationed in Iraq to balance its military budget. It is hard to believe, however, that the president does not grasp the enormity of his errors or their consequences. The impact on the domestic economy is likely to be staggering. Paul Bremer told the *Washington Post* that reconstruction alone will cost "several tens of billions of dollars," describing the resources required to rebuild Iraq as "almost impossible to exaggerate." And that does not include the costs of the military operation, which is running at about a billion dollars a week—almost twice the amount estimated by the Pentagon in April.

This was a war that was supposed to mostly pay for itself. With victory round the corner in March, Paul Wolfowitz told Congress, "We're dealing with a country that can really finance its own reconstruction, and relatively soon." His boss Donald Rumsfeld would not commit himself to an estimate, but assured members that frozen Iraqi assets, Iraqi oil revenue, and U.S. allies would fund the bulk of the reconstruction. "When it comes to reconstruction, before we turn to the American taxpayer, we will turn first to the resources of the Iraqi government and the international community," he said. Like the administration's other rosy predictions, this scenario, too, fell by the wayside after the war. It became increasingly apparent that Iraq's oil refineries were in no shape to subsidize the reconstruction. Early in the war, independent experts had cautioned the administration that a return to prewar production of two and a half to three million barrels a day would require at least five billion dollars of investment and take several years. They have turned out to be right. Not only was Iraq's oil infrastructure in a state of disrepair, but the subsequent sabotage in August of the Kirkuk-Ceyhan pipeline, Iraq's second largest, dashed any remaining hope of an oil dividend. Bremer was finally forced to admit that the U.S. will not be able to restore pre-war levels of production until October 2004. Worse, even those revenues will not be sufficient to pay for the reconstruction.

Faced with this financial train wreck, the administration's response has been to continually stonewall. When asked to provide an estimate in July, White House Budget Director Joshua Bolten simply told Congress that the administration will not ask for funds in the fiscal 2004 budget for either military or reconstruction costs because it didn't know what they would be. Wolfowitz in his response chose instead to speak at length on Iraq's significance as "the central battle in the global war on terror." Fellow Republican and Senate Foreign Relations Committee chair Richard Lugar spent his entire allotment of time imploring Bolten and Wolfowitz to develop a realistic, long-term budget for Iraq's reconstruction, but to no avail. The figures provided by Bremer remained equally vague—"tens of billions," "well above $50 billion, $60 billion, maybe $100 billion," and so on.

Faced with a massive economic fallout and rising casualty rate that could jeopardize its reelection prospects, the Bush administration has not changed course. Instead, it has fallen back on its tried-and-tested rhetoric of terrorism. In August, General John Abizaid, the head of the U.S. Central Command, echoed the White House's spin on the disastrous situation in Iraq. "I think Iraq is at the center of the global war on terrorism," he told reporters, confirming the increased involvement of Islamic terrorists in the guerrilla war. The attack on the UN headquarters and a brutal suicide bombing in Jerusalem occurred on the same day, allowing the White House to make all the misleading connections. Bush marshaled the standard clichés in his "war on terror" repertoire—"Our will cannot be shaken; we will persevere through every hardship"—in the hope that once again the terrorist card would let him off the hook. A senior Bush official told reporters, "It's emblematic of the kind of problem that we are fighting. There is a movement out there that simply doesn't want to see a different future for the Middle East, and everybody is beginning to understand that."

Faced with increasing skepticism regarding its claims about an Al Qaeda–Saddam connection, the administration seized on the two tragedies for a macabre "I told you so" display. "Those who said there was no link between Iraq and the war on terror were dead wrong," said another White House honcho. Better yet, the Bush team began to argue that being a "terrorist magnet" was in fact a smart move. Ricardo Sanchez, commander of the coalition ground forces, declared, "[This] is what I would call a terrorist magnet where America, being present here in Iraq, creates a target of opportunity, if you will, but this is exactly where we want to fight them. We want to fight them here, we prepared for them, and this will prevent the American people from having to go through their attacks back in the United States." Bremer and other Bush officials studiously parroted this argument in the following weeks.

The reality is that the billions of dollars and hundreds of lives lost in the Iraq War have left Americans seemingly more vulnerable than ever. Not only has the war in Iraq not advanced the fight against terrorism, it has helped Al Qaeda regroup and recover. Flynt Leverett, a former director at the National Security Council in the Bush White House, told NBC in July, "There were decisions made to take key assets, human assets, technical assets, out of the theater in Afghanistan in order to position them for the campaign to unseat Saddam." While Iraq remains in chaos, terrorist cells are regrouping in Afghanistan and along its border with Iran. There is no doubt that many of them will try and find their way into Iraq. The White House is right in describing the U.S. presence as a "terrorist magnet." As former Clinton national security official Jessica Stern pointed out in the *New York Times* on August 20, 2003, "America has taken a country that was not a terrorist threat and turned it into one." The president, who taunted the terrorists to "bring 'em on" from the safety of the White House, has turned his soldiers into human bait.

Poorly manned and equipped, they are mired in a country that may become the epicenter of a global war.

Senator Robert Byrd wrote in the *Washington Post* in August, "What has become tragically clear is that the United States has no strong plan for turning Iraq over to the Iraqi people and is quickly losing even its ability to maintain order. The administration is stumbling through the dark, hoping by luck to find the lighted path to peace and stability." But to find its way, the Bush White House must first summon up not just courage and wisdom, but also that most undervalued quality: humility.

Iraq As a Democratic Model

"America believes that all people are entitled to hope and human rights, to the nonnegotiable demands of human dignity. People everywhere prefer freedom to slavery; prosperity to squalor; self-government to the rule of terror and torture. America is a friend to the people of Iraq. Our demands are directed only at the regime that enslaves them and threatens us. When these demands are met, the first and greatest benefit will come to Iraqi men, women, and children. The oppression of Kurds, Assyrians, Turkomans, Shia, Sunnis, and others will be lifted. The long captivity of Iraq will end, and an era of new hope will begin."

—President Bush, October 7, 2002

"Americans will support a Pax Americana only if it promotes values that they believe to be shared by all humanity; but it is just such a peace that the majority of mankind will find most oppressive. In the volatile mix of geopolitical calculation and messianic enthusiasm that is presently shaping America's foreign policy, it is not American realpolitik that the world most resents. It is American universalism."

—John Gray, *Al Qaeda and What It Means to Be Modern*

IN THE FIRST WEEK OF April, after carefully crafted U.S. public relations were foiled for weeks by photos of sandstorms, friendly-fire mayhem, American POWs, and terrified and dead Iraqi civilians, the White House finally got a shot it must have hoped would come sooner: U.S. soldiers lounging in easy chairs in one of Saddam Hussein's palaces.

"Saddam Sat Here," read the headline on the *San Francisco Chronicle's* website. The symbolism was great—the United States was now sitting where Hussein had, ruling by force alone a violent, fractious, and ruined Arab Muslim country with a tortured past and an uncertain future. The occupation was to be the true Battle of Iraq 2003, and the odds were long.

This battle was for the hearts and minds of Iraqis, Americans, and the rest of the world, and the traps into which the invaders would fall would turn out to be much more dangerous than those posed by an ill-armed, poorly led regime. As an occupying army in a nation with which it has no cultural affinity, the U.S. has to accomplish a miracle: build from scratch a functioning democracy in a country full of sharply divided nationalist, religious, and tribal passions and with no history of political freedom—and do it by force without antagonizing the populace.

The price of failure? More terrorism, more death of innocents, more damage to the U.S. economy, possibly even full-blown civil or regional war. The United States has won nothing yet.

■ ■ ■

"If military action is necessary, the United States and our allies will help the Iraqi people rebuild their economy, and create the institutions of liberty in a unified Iraq at peace with its neighbors."

—President Bush, October 7, 2002, in a speech in Cincinnati

"We will remain in Iraq as long as necessary, and not a day more."

—President Bush, February 26, 2003, at the American Enterprise Institute

THE UNITED STATES, if not every country, needs a moral and strategic argument for going to war, to placate its pretensions both to ultra-pragmatism and city-on-the-hill purity. And, as Norman Mailer argues in his book *Why We Are at War,* this may be especially true at this moment:

"This war [on terror], if it proliferates over the next decade, could prove worse in one respect than any conflict we have yet experienced," writes Mailer. "It is that we will never know just what we are fighting for. It is not enough to say we are against terrorism. Of course we are. In America, who is not? But terrorism compared to more conventional kinds of war is formless, and it is hard to feel righteous when in combat with a void, for then the action smacks of rage and relative impotence, a frightful combination that deprives warrior and citizen alike any sense of virtue. Be it said, the sense of national virtue is crucial to waging a war."

For Iraq, weapons of mass destruction and antiterrorism were the advertised strategic goals, while building a new "free and democratic Iraq" was the moral one. Zigzagging back and forth between these two proved a very useful dodge; whenever one was challenged, the other would be moved to the fore: You don't think our intelligence on Iraq's unconventional weapons is very solid? How dare you make the Iraqi people suffer under that tyrant for another minute! You wonder if America is the right country to reform the Arab world by force? Well, fine, if you want to wake up one morning to the sight of a mushroom cloud over our nation's capital, that's your business.

"The administration short-circuited the discussion of whether war was necessary because some of its most powerful members felt it was the best option—ostensibly because they had deluded themselves into believing that they could easily impose flowering democracies on the region," wrote Joe Wilson, former U.S. diplomat in Iraq and whistle-blower in the Iraq/Niger uranium myth, in an essay published in the *San Jose Mercury News* and on AlterNet in mid-September 2003.

Flowering or not, propagating the idea that the American military could unlock the door to prosperity, freedom, and true democracy for a country as large, complex, and fundamentally different from our own as Iraq was a farcical act of hubris. It was also a tremendous lie of omission: The president told us that we could deliver a miracle to the Iraqi people—and the region as a whole—that would forever grant the venture an angelic, altruistic sheen while simultaneously making our children's world safer. We could, should, and would, he argued, give these poor people the gift of freedom, of which our own country is the sacred repository.

In other words, we weren't conquering Iraq, we were "liberating" it. As Colin Powell described it dramatically upon his first visit to occupied Iraq: "We are not occupiers. We have come under a legal term having to do with occupation under international law, but we came as liberators. We have experience being liberators. Our history over the last 50, 60 years is quite clear. We have liberated a number of countries, and we do not own one square foot of any of those countries, except where we bury our dead." (Powell apparently forgot that we possess massive military bases in Germany, South Korea, and various other countries.)

But when the president said, on the eve of war, that we would stay in Iraq "as long as necessary," he was making a commitment on our behalf that goes far beyond some romantic ideal of sending in the noble calvary to reinstall the rightful king, before returning to our pastoral pursuits. We are not Robin Hood, aiding Richard the Lionhearted and then returning to the forest.

Rather, Bush has led us blindly into a much more involved position, one that is looking more and more untenable. Pursuing what even his ally Richard Perle called "a very risky venture," the president has thrown the dice for us—risking our money, our young people's lives, our credibility with the rest of the world. As we have seen, it was a commitment that would put an enormous burden on American servicemen and service-women, as well as United States taxpayers, in the first six months alone.

Yet before this massive gamble, Bush provided almost no details to the American people about the expected costs such a commitment entailed, how such an ambitious program would be carried out, the risks involved, or the likelihood of success or failure. What little leaked out about the administration's postwar vision involved a quick downsizing of the U.S. troop commitment by fall and a contradictory uber-role for a Defense Department–led interim government, rather than one run under UN auspices. Also rumored were a prominent role for Iraqi exiles in general and Ahmed Chalabi in particular, a man who hadn't been on the ground in Iraq since 1958 at age 13 and whom the CIA had deemed a flake some time ago.

No matter, though, Bush assured the conservative guests at the American Enterprise Institute's annual dinner on the eve of war. "America has made and kept this kind of commitment before—in the peace that followed a world war. After defeating enemies, we did not leave behind occupying armies, we left constitutions and parliaments. We established an atmosphere of safety, in which responsible, reform-minded local leaders could build lasting institutions of freedom. In societies that once bred fascism and militarism, liberty found a permanent home."

Put this way, it sounds almost easy, as if you could toss civics textbooks from the back of the tank and democracy would just sprout. Yet Bush is talking here about Japan and Germany, two heavily industrialized, culturally homogenous nations which were occupied for years while being granted enormous economic aid.

Was the United States really prepared for such a commitment in 2003? After all, it has been nearly 50 years without such an effort, unless you count the failed attempt to keep Vietnam from being run by Communists, or our ambitious and failed attempt under Clinton to remake the tiny island-nation of Haiti. And, if we were that serious, that willing to spend and suffer and stay the course, would we be able to repeat that long ago success in Muslim Iraq, a nation riven by ethnic, religious, and geographical divides sitting in the middle of a contentious and unstable region?

Bush had a preemptive answer for that one, playing the "politically correct" card: "There was a time when many said that the cultures of Japan and Germany were incapable of sustaining democratic values. Well, they were wrong. Some say the same of Iraq today. They are mistaken. The nation of Iraq—with its proud heritage, abundant resources, and skilled and educated people—is fully capable of moving toward democracy and living in freedom."

Still, many of those not on the White House payroll who nevertheless supported the idea that America should lead a renaissance of Babylonia were less sanguine about what was involved:

"Freeing the Iraqi people from Saddam Hussein's depredations would be justification enough for his overthrow *if the American people were willing to pay the price of doing so,*" said Neal Pollack [italics added].

"President George W. Bush has often said that America wants to help build democracy in Iraq. He has also said that America will hand over power to Iraqis as soon as possible," wrote Fareed Zakaria in an essay for *Newsweek* in late April 2003, adapted from his book *The Future of Freedom.* "These are, of course, the politically correct things to say. Washington does not want to look like an occupying power. But the history of political and economic reform around the world suggest that building democracy in Iraq will require a prolonged American or international presence. We can leave fast or we can nurture democracy, but we cannot do both."

Some prominent neoconservatives opine that while a democratic revolution sparked by regime change in Iraq might be plausible and positive, it would nevertheless still be a vast improvement on the current prickly state of affairs in the region if it would all return to a sort of precolonial, pre-national state of tribal and religious anarchy, where everybody would be too busy watching their neighbor to hassle Israel.

"A more cynical reading of the agenda of certain Bush advisers could conclude that the Balkanization of Iraq was always an acceptable outcome, because Israel would then find itself surrounded by small Arab countries worried about each other instead of forming a solid block against Israel," Joe Wilson wrote. "After all, Iraq was an artificial country that had always had a troublesome history." This would help explain why many conservatives allied with the White House have argued strenuously for the need to decapitate or undermine the autocratic but nationalist regimes of Syria and Iran, as well as Iraq, with little explanation for what would take its place.

Whether or not the president himself wants a flourishing or floundering Middle East is unknown. But reading between the lines of his speeches, it is clear that one possible outcome for a post-Hussein Iraq that the president repeatedly hinted at was far less ambitious than what Bush laid out for the AEI.

"We'll help that nation to build a just government, after decades of brutal dictatorship," Bush said on March 6, 2003, before going on to hedge quite a bit. "The form and leadership of that government is for the Iraqi people to choose. Anything they choose will be better than the misery and torture and murder they have known under Saddam Hussein."

"Some worry that a change of leadership in Iraq could create instability and make the situation worse," Bush later told America on October 7, 2002. "The situation could hardly get worse, for world security and for the people of Iraq. The lives of Iraqi citizens would improve dramatically if Saddam Hussein were no longer in power, just as the lives of Afghanistan's citizens improved after the Taliban."

Such statements are problematic for many reasons. First of all, it is never wise to say "things can't get worse," as they often can and do. Furthermore, comparing this post-Hussein Iraq to post-Taliban Afghanistan should be terrifying for any Iraqi who hopes the United States can make good on its promise of midwifing a prosperous and democratic Iraq. While some people in Kabul have benefited from the lifting of the more bizarre restrictions of life under the Taliban, Afghanistan today, two years removed from the U.S. invasion, is a complete and utter mess—violent, poor, and ruled by a patchwork quilt of warlords and, in some areas, resurgent Taliban.

In his book *The Threatening Storm: The Case for Invading Iraq*, published before the invasion, Neal Pollack looked at what he referred to as the "Pragmatic Approach":

The Pragmatic Approach proceeds from the fundamental assumption that building a new, stable Iraq is going to be a long and costly process—if it can succeed at all—and therefore that the United States should be looking for a practical short-term solution, rather than a Wilsonian long-term one. . . .

Under a worst-case scenario, a new dictator would probably emerge who, while unappealing, would maintain order and who would likely be someone with whom the United States could work. We probably would not help in the creation of such a dictator, but we would probably accept him as long as his methods for consolidating power were mostly peaceful and he observed a "decent interval" after the withdrawal of U.S. forces before doing so. In effect, the United States would be acquiescing to the establishment of just one more Arab autocracy that, hopefully, would be no more problematic than Hosni Mubarak's Egypt—although it would be hard to prevent it from turning out like Assad's Syria, Qadhafi's Libya, or Saddam's Iraq all over again.

That doesn't sound good, does it? Hundreds of billions of dollars, hundreds of dead soldiers, and thousands of wounded . . . for Saddam II? You can see where Pollack was heading: "The rebuilding of Iraq cannot be an afterthought to a policy of regime change. Instead, it must be a central element in U.S. preparations. It is likely to be the most important and difficult part of the policy, and we would be living with the results or suffering from the consequences for many decades to come."

This squares with the conventional wisdom in the United States before the war, which had always predicted that our commitment to "nation-building" in oil-rich Iraq was much higher than in Afghanistan, since it is a far more advanced, strategic country and one of great significance in the Arab world. In other words, we were told time and again, we've got to get it right in Iraq. This would seem to have precluded the Afghanistan approach of minimal aid, minimal help. (So much for moral consistency as the basis for foreign policy: There are actually four million more people in Afghanistan than in Iraq, and their average life expectancy is twenty years shorter.)

If the White House was sending mixed messages on our long-term commitment to Iraq, the confusion was manifested in its policy. Rumsfeld's fighting vigorously for a smaller troop commitment later would make it hard to insure the safety of those who wanted to take part in any political or civic processes. The slaying of the country's most important Shiite cleric was a huge setback, for example. Impatience with the UN and "Old Europe" meant we would be going it alone later, without the experience, troops, or money of either. The early decision to disband the Iraqi military and purge the state bureaucracy of huge numbers of Ba'ath party members was designed to promote democracy, but left a huge vacuum.

In the middle of what was proving to be a very dispiriting summer for both occupiers and the occupied, Bush urged patience: "I remind some of my friends that it took us awhile to go from the Articles of Confederation to the United States Constitution. Even our own experiment with democracy didn't happen overnight. I never have expected Thomas Jefferson to emerge in Iraq in a 90-day period." He still made no real effort to explain to Americans why things seemed to be spiraling out of control.

On September 7, he made his request for the staggering sum of $87 billion combined for Afghanistan and Iraq, added on to the $79 billion already budgeted. A week later, Colin Powell rebuked French and Iraqi pressure for a speedier timetable for handing over power. "We're not hanging on for the sake of hanging on," said Powell while in Baghdad, after meeting with the Iraqi Governing Council handpicked by the United States months earlier. "The worst thing that could happen is for us to push this process too quickly."

The decision seemed to have been made: We are going to stay in Iraq for a long, long time.

IN MANY WAYS, the dangerous and faulty promise that American military, economic, and political power could be employed directly to create a peaceful citadel of democracy in the Middle East that would be friendly to the West, join us in the "war on terror," and generally behave in a way deemed civilized by those writing editorials for American newspapers, was spread as much by outspoken liberals as the neoconservative Republicans who dominate the Bush White House. In a very real sense, a motley brigade of liberal commentators and politicians, led by *New York Times* flagship columnist Thomas Friedman and the majority of the Democratic Party candidates for president in 2004, acted as a sort of "fifth column" for the Bush administration's misinformation campaign.

These men and women, whether for political, career, emotional, or intellectual reasons, had decided to support the Bush war while picking and choosing which of its arguments to believe, the better to keep their self-respect and impression of independence. "Well, I don't believe Hussein is behind 9/11," one would say, "but I'm worried he has nukes and he's a terrible tyrant." Another would emphasize the importance of "bringing the Arab world in to the Age of Enlightenment," while playing down the WMD angle as overblown. Everybody agreed that no matter what happened after the Ba'ath thugs were thrown from their palaces, it would inevitably be better for the world and Iraqis.

"As far as I'm concerned, we do not need to find any weapons of mass destruction to justify this war," wrote Friedman in April 2003. "Mr. Bush doesn't owe the world any explanation for missing chemical weapons (even if it turns out that the White House hyped this issue.)"

A funny thing happened, though, after the invasion and occupation of Iraq was accomplished: Friedman, Dick Gephardt, et al, realized they had no tanks at their disposal, nor civil engineers, military police, UN-friendly diplomats, and the rest. In other words, they didn't control the United States government or wield its power. Having gotten in bed with a bear, they woke up sometime in the summer of 2003 complaining they didn't like being hugged so hard. Why weren't things going according to plan?

"America broke Iraq; now America owns Iraq, and it owns the primary responsibility for normalizing it," wrote Friedman on April 9, 2003, after describing scenes of squalor and describing Iraqis as being "in a pre-political, primordial state of nature." Only a few weeks into the occupation and he was sounding worried, almost plaintive. "If the water doesn't flow, if the food doesn't arrive, if the rains don't come, and if the sun doesn't shine, it's now America's fault. We'd better get used to it, we'd better make things right, we'd better do it soon, and we'd better get all the help we can get."

Since Friedman's descriptions of the "owner's" responsibilities to these savages—White Man's Burden, perhaps?—sound more like those usually ascribed to God, it is perhaps not surprising that as of six months later we have failed so miserably on all counts.

"We are so caught up with our own story of 'America's liberation of Iraq,'" said Friedman in April, apparently without irony, "and the Arab TV networks are so caught up with their own story of 'America's occupation of Iraq,' that everyone seems to have lost sight of the real lives of Iraqis."

Ah, yes, the "real lives of Iraqis," for whom the Bush administration said—sometimes, when it was convenient and other rationales were falling apart—it was doing all this. What could those "real" Iraqis want? Simple, Bush has said over and over again, it's very simple: They want freedom. The real question is, however, do we sincerely want them to have it, since they may use it in ways we don't like?

■   ■   ■

"It is presumptuous and insulting to suggest that a whole region of the world—or the one-fifth of humanity that is Muslim—is somehow untouched by the most basic aspirations of life. Human cultures can be vastly different. Yet the human heart desires the same good things, everywhere on earth. In our desire to be safe from brutal and bullying oppression, human beings are the same. In our desire to care for our children and give them a better life, we are the same. For these fundamental reasons, freedom and democracy will always and everywhere have greater appeal than the slogans of hatred and the tactics of terror."

—President Bush, February 26, 2003, at the American Enterprise Institute

IN THE BOOK *Al Qaeda and What It Means to Be Modern,* scholar John Gray pinpoints a conflict inherent to America's self-image that explains a lot about our love-hate relationship with nation-building in far-off lands about which we know basically nothing.

"On the one hand, many Americans believe that all human beings are Americans under the skin. On the other hand, they have long viewed the world—especially the Old World of Europe—as corrupt, possibly beyond redemption," Gray writes. "Contradictory as these American attitudes seem, they flow from a common premise. Either the world will evolve to the point at which it mirrors America, or else it can safely be left to its own devices."

Al Qaeda's success, Gray argues, has destroyed this assumption. Yet now the United States is again trying to remake the world in our image, as formulated in the Bush administration's National Security Policy submitted to Congress in September 2002. "Declaring that the era of deterrence and containment was over, the paper committed the U.S.— acting alone if necessary—to a far-reaching preemptive campaign against terrorism. At the same time, the paper includes a classical Wilsonian declaration of American universalism. American institutions are the only possible model for the world, it declares; the twentieth century ended with 'a decisive victory for the forces of freedom—and a single sustainable model for national success: freedom, democracy, and free enterprise.'"

Yet, what if, for example, Iraqi Muslim fundamentalists prove as successful at the polls as radicals in Algeria, where the U.S. only mildly rebuked a repressive regime for smashing a popularly elected but theocratic opposition? Or if the new Iraq followed the path of repressive Pakistan, where the population is inclined to obliterate any wall between state and church, could Bush spin this as a victory for democracy?

And what if a new Iraq decided it still wanted nuclear weapons? As weapons expert Joseph Cirincione of the Carnegie Institute points out, "Even if democratic transformations sweep the Middle East, a new Iraq and a new Iran might still want nuclear weapons as long as Israel has them and as long as such weapons are seen as the currency of great powers. The Iranian nuclear program began under the Shah, when the United States sold that nation its first reactor; that program will likely continue under future governments unless regional dynamics change fundamentally."

Or, what if a new regime tolerated or even encouraged the kind of ethnic cleansing common to a nation divided by competing tribal, clan, and religious loyalties and arbitrarily packed together by previous colonialist rulers. Would Rumsfeld, who famously said that "freedom is untidy" when questioned about postwar looting, see such human rights abuses as part of the unruly joy of freedom?

As Zakaria pointed out in *Newsweek*, there is "a general rise of identity politics in the Arab world. The failure of regimes like Saddam's—originally Western-styled, socialist, secular—has led people to see Islam as their salvation and to seek comfort in their tribal and ethnic backgrounds. Young democracies have a very poor record of handling ethnic and religious conflict. . . . Elections require that politicians compete for votes. In societies without strong traditions of tolerance and multiethnic groups, the easiest way to get support is by appealing to people's most basic affiliations—racial, religious, ethnic. Once one group wins, it usually excludes the other from power. The opposition becomes extreme, sometimes violent."

And, finally, what if this new democracy elects leaders who are skeptical of the United States and its motives? Who perhaps see designs on their oil, or a threat to local economies and fortunes by multinational corporations?

"In the last analysis, the world will not accept a Pax Americana because it resists the imposition of American values," concludes Gray. "For many Americans, this may seem paradoxical. Are not American ideals shared by all of humankind? The answer is that insofar as they are American, they are not. Beyond its shores, no one accepts America's claim to be the model for a universal civilization."

WESTERNERS ARE FIRM in their belief that democracy looks a certain way—the way we do it. But if the definition of democracy is merely a government representative of the people, there are many ways to get there. For example, in many well-functioning societies, whether tribal, theocratic, or anarchistic, having a set of rules that all members of society recognize, investing in esteemed elders the roles of judges and arbiters, and establishing ritualized forums within which to air and work out grievances insure that conflict is dealt with in nonviolent, mutually-beneficial ways. In one of the many ironies of the U.S. invasion of Iraq, our complete failure to create or prop up a national government allowed ad-hoc local committees to spring up across the country to fill the void, almost always based on tribal or religious lines.

Nationally, however, things languished terribly, with almost no progress being made in six months. As of this writing, in October 2003, the so-called Iraqi Governing Council, 25 individuals handpicked by the United States, governs nothing, and many of its members are afraid for their lives, having gone public with their concerns that the United States is not providing them with adequate security. On September 25, 2003, Akila al-Hashemi, one of three women on the Governing Council, died of gunshot wounds she received five days earlier in an ambush.

No elections are planned, no constitutional committee has been appointed, no timeline has been approved. Ministers have been appointed, but they are not in control of anything of import. There is simply no there there, in the words of Gertrude Stein, outside of the United States' administration. Fear of the "Saddamists" is so prevalent, according to Friedman, that "Iraq's silent majority" is unwilling to pub-licly express its support for the occupation.

"The big thing that has happened in Iraq, which you can really feel when you're there, is that there is a 100 percent correlation of interests between America's aspirations for Iraq and the aspirations of Iraq's silent majority," Friedman wrote on September 21, 2003. "We both want the same thing for Iraq—that it not become Iran, that it not become Saddam, but that it become a decent, modern-looking Iraqi alternative. This overlap of aspirations is hugely important."

Yet, he cautions, "Friedman's first rule of Middle East reporting: What people tell you in private is irrelevant. All that matters is what they will defend in public. And when I see Iraqis defending our shared aspi-rations—with both their words and their lives—my optimism will know no bounds and every glass will look full." And he went on to bemoan the fact that so little progress has been made on developing Iraqi-run insti-tutions, especially security structures like a new army. "The war has to be finished, but we can't be the ones to finish it. This is a purely urban fight, and if we try to finish it alone what will happen is more of what's hap-pened in the past two weeks—fatal blunders. We just accidentally killed 10 Iraqi policemen in one town and gunned down a 14-year-old Iraqi boy in another who was part of a wedding party firing guns in celebra-tion. Non-Arabic-speaking Americans cannot fight an urban war in Iraq. Forget it. We must get off this course immediately."

Hopefully Friedman was not holding his breath. Colin Powell, in his first visit to the country in mid-September and responding to reports that France was urging the United States to hand off control of Iraq's political transition to the United Nations, explained that this was impossible because "there is not yet a functioning government that you can turn authority over to."

Of course, such an admission half a year after you've taken over a country is perhaps the best argument for bringing in the UN. Nevertheless, according to the *New York Times*, "the overriding message the secretary said he had heard from Iraqis at the Governing Council and at the Baghdad City Council was gratitude for what the United States had done in taking over Iraq."

(Maybe Powell should listen to more of Friedman's irritated advice: "Whenever senior U.S. officials tell me about Iraqis who thanked them, with tears in their eyes, for getting rid of Saddam, I have a simple response: Could you please ask those Iraqis to say it in public, in Arabic, on Al-Jazeera TV? There's been way too little of that.")

All in all, it was on odd visit for Powell. Rather than being greeted by cheering throngs, Powell was kept indoors under extremely tight security. Normally famous for his charm, he sounded testy in many of his comments—at one point lashing out at the French, saying, "We were right, they were wrong, and I am here." And while he said he was very happy with all the positive things happening, he again grew defensive when asked if he might be getting only half the story.

"I don't know if I will have the opportunity to go around town and ask people if they are unhappy, so come forward," he said. "But I think I've been around long enough to understand the things I'm being told and to see behind the things I'm being told."

The defensiveness was understandable. To U.S. newspaper readers, things in Iraq seemed to be going just awful, and for some analysts, things were even worse than they looked.

"There is every indication that the Americans really don't get it," wrote journalist Geov Parrish on September 4, 2003. "Far beyond the casual arrogance of Bush, Bremer, and America's other CNN talking heads, our culture, our history, our way of social and political thinking is so profoundly different from that of most Iraqis that an event like the Najaf bombing [that killed Iraqi cleric Ayatollah Muhammad Bakr al-Hakim and dozens of other Shiite worshippers] can be just another headline in this country, and yet profoundly transformative among Iraqis.

"This has been an attack and assassination that underscores, for a deeply religious Shiite public, that the Americans don't get it—they're secular nonbelievers, who didn't respect the Shiites' religion, temple, and leaders enough to have prevented this attack from happening, who are constitutionally incapable of such respect."

Those neoconservatives who had supported the war scrapped around for some good news. AEI's Danielle Pletka wrote happily in mid-September that attacks on U.S. troops had fallen slightly, from 25 a week to just 15. Yet within days of her optimistic op-ed, several more U.S. soldiers had been killed in ambushes, another deadly bomb went off near the UN's offices in Baghdad, U.S. soldiers bombed a family's home, and the head of the American-appointed Iraqi Governing Council, Ahmed Chalabi, was demanding Washington greatly accelerate its handover of power to Iraqis.

In many ways, the United States is in a fatal bind in Iraq—one Zakaria, who supported the invasion, was honest enough to acknowledge. "Until a legitimate Iraqi government has been formed—until national elections—the United States will play the role of honest broker among the various factions. And yet this is going to be called colonialism," he wrote presciently back in April. "This then is the paradox: To build democracy in Iraq, the United States must stay on, but to demonstrate that it is not a colonial power, it must leave."

For Zakaria, "The solution lies in involving other countries in this process. To the extent that the United States can make the assistance to Iraq multilateral, all the better." In September, President Bush made extremely cautious noises to the effect that he would now be open to getting some help from the rest of the world. As of this writing, however, nothing concrete has emerged and the U.S., along with its sidekick Britain, still straddles what can only be called a quagmire, not entirely unlike that of the West Bank or even, yes, Vietnam.

"I RECENTLY REREAD Bernard Fall's book on Vietnam, *Street Without Joy,*" wrote Colin Powell in his 1995 autobiography, immediately after describing how a young soldier had died in his arms fighting a war that had long ago seemed to lose its purpose. "[French war correspondent] Fall makes painfully clear that we had almost no understanding of what we had gotten ourselves into. I cannot help thinking that if President Kennedy or President Johnson had spent a quiet weekend at Camp David reading that perceptive book, they would have returned to the White House Monday morning and immediately started to figure out a way to extricate us from the quicksand of Vietnam."

For critics of the war on Iraq, the irony of this statement by Bush's secretary of state is overwhelming; substitute Iraq for Vietnam and Bush for Kennedy and Johnson and you have the current situation in a nutshell. Powell continued:

"War should be the politics of last resort. And when we go to war, we should have a purpose that our people understand and support; we should mobilize the country's resources to fulfill that mission and then go in to win. In Vietnam, we had entered into a halfhearted half-war, with much of the nation opposed or indifferent, while a small fraction carried the burden."

Was the invasion of Iraq the politics of last resort? No, and the world told us so. Did the American people understand and support the invasion of Iraq? How could they, when they were misled by our government about the threat we faced and the difficulty of the challenge we were accepting? And did we mobilize the country's resources? Well, yes, but not only couldn't we afford the bill when it came due but it was not going to be enough to fulfill the fantastic promises we had made.

"In time, just as I came to reexamine my feelings about the war, the army, as an institution, would do the same thing," continued Powell. "We accepted that we had been sent to pursue a policy that had become bankrupt. Our political leaders had led us into a war for the one-size-fits-all rationale of anticommunism, which was only a partial fit in Vietnam, where the war had its own historical roots in nationalism, anti-colonialism, and civil strife beyond the East-West conflict."

Here, simply substitute the word antiterrorism for anticommunism and you have as apt a description of occupied Iraq as you'll find any-where. Finally, Powell concluded his summary thoughts on his tour of duty in Vietnam, "Many of my generation, the career captains, majors, and lieutenant colonels seasoned in that war, vowed that when our turn came to call the shots we would not quietly acquiesce in halfhearted warfare for half-baked reasons that the American people could not understand or support. If we could make good on that promise to our-selves, to the civilian leadership, and to the country, then the sacrifices of Vietnam would not have been in vain."

SOMEWHERE IN THE DEPTHS of your local Barnes and Noble store there is likely a moderately sized hardcover book sitting forlornly in the Middle East History section with a bright-red cover optimistically enti-tled *The New Iraq: Rebuilding the Country for Its People, the Middle East, and the World.*

The book, written by Joseph Braude, published in 2003 and endorsed on its back by the odd couple of ex–CIA Director R. James Woolsey and legendary First Amendment journalist Nat Hentoff, is an astonishingly detailed step-by-step program for rebuilding every aspect of Iraq after an invasion and occupation.

"A superb guide for the rebirth of the great civilization of Iraq by one who knows the country, its history, and its culture intimately. It's all here: how to resuscitate the judicial system, the army, the economy, even the cinema," says Woolsey, in his plug.

And indeed, the book, written by an American of Jewish-Iraqi descent, is lively, enlightening, and earnest, rather self-consciously positioning itself as a guidebook to the policymaker, NGO worker, or entrepreneur who has just entered a free, proud, and rebuilding post-Saddam Iraq. The author clearly has a deep appreciation for his parents' homeland and writes well; if one reads even one chapter he or she will likely have a better understanding of the place than 99 percent of American politicians.

And yet, in the context of the past year, what would otherwise read like hopeful optimism sounds rather more like a long "thumbsucker," to use the cruel argot of the newsroom, full of sentimental nostalgia and glib liberal solutions to problems long deemed intractable.

"The path to the new Iraq is not without its roadblocks," Braude allows in the book's prologue, which describes in detail the peaceful if hardscrabble life of an Iraqi refugee camp in Saudi Arabia. "But once Iraqis stabilize and liberate their own capacities and infrastructure, they will turn outward. Then the modern standard-bearers of the world's oldest civilization will use their extraordinary talents as entrepreneurs and facilitators to shine light on knowledge and information gaps all over the Middle East and beyond."

When sweeping prescriptions and bold predictions like those Braude—and Zakaria and Pollack, for that matter—describe are combined with a healthy dose of naïveté about the larger world's good will and good faith, the result fits well in a long tradition of well-meaning American arrogance perfectly captured by Graham Greene's mythic depiction of the "Quiet American."

The sad fact is that the notion that Iraq could have its own path, its own history—let alone that 7,000 years ago this land was the cradle of civilization—is not likely to occur to Americans, not ever. Our earnest innocence and can-do, we-can-fix-anything optimism are what our entertainment industry markets so successfully around the world, but they are also the perennial seeds of disaster as we blithely rearrange corners of the planet we can only pretend to understand.

Interventionists love to point over and over again to World War II as the model for successful American war-fighting and nation-building. But WWII is the exception to the rule, on all counts. World War I, Korea, Vietnam, Lebanon, Panama, Somalia, Afghanistan, and now Iraq are the norm: wars of great moral ambiguity and even more uncertain outcomes.

And as with those wars, we once again only find out how bloody and ambiguous the situation is once we're stuck there because our leaders seem unable or unwilling to speak the truth to us before it is too late.

Conclusion

SO OUR PRESIDENT LIED. He did so repeatedly, consistently, and thus far, without remorse. So what? It isn't the first time that a politician has lied to the people, nor will it be the last. Some presidents lie about war and others about sex. To be caught in a lie has rarely been sufficient reason to lose trust in a leader.

In an article for AlterNet, linguist George Lakoff argues, "The most startling finding is that, in considering whether a statement is a lie, the *least* important consideration for most people is whether it is true!" The more important standards applied by Americans, Lakoff says, is the nature of the lie. Lies borne of self-delusion, of good intent, or of error are more forgivable than willful manipulation in the cause of a dishonest agenda.

To what category do the five lies in this book belong? Busted on its claims about Saddam's nuclear program and arsenal of bio-chemical weapons, the administration now alleges that it was, at worst, misled by faulty intelligence and even false information planted by Saddam Hussein himself. But as we've shown, there is no doubt that the Bush White House deliberately deployed intelligence it knew was thoroughly discredited regarding the alleged imminent threat posed by Saddam. In fact, the Pentagon's Office of Special Plans was created precisely to "find" evidence to support a preconceived plan to attack Iraq—a plan that was already in place and ready to go hours after the Twin Towers collapsed.

The same is true of the lie linking Al Qaeda to Saddam Hussein. The war on terror was not the cause but an excuse to invade and occupy Iraq.

168 THE FIVE BIGGEST LIES BUSH TOLD US ABOUT IRAQ

While the administration finally backed away in September 2003 from claims linking Saddam specifically to the 9/11 attacks, it is now reshaping this lie to create political cover for the disastrous consequences of this war without the slightest trace of shame. Sure, there might not have been any terrorists in Iraq before, but they are there now. Bush's claim about Iraq as a hotbed of terrorism has turned into a self-fulfilling prophecy.

Lakoff writes, "These have been among the administration's defenses. The good cause: liberating Iraq. The faulty information: from the CIA. The emphasis: enthusiasm for a great cause." Never mind, insists Bush, if things have not gone to plan, and the situation in Iraq is less than ideal, it is all for a good cause: to fight terrorism and bring democracy to Iraq. Herein lies the core of the biggest bait and switch operation in recent history—in the hidden cause for this war. This was not the wrong war fought for the right reasons. In this case, the ends were every bit as nefarious as the means used to achieve them.

If fighting terrorism is more the effect of, than the reason for, the invasion, then liberating Iraq was never really part of the game plan. As we've shown, the Bush administration never once made a good faith effort to serve the interests of the Iraqi people. The Iraqis, like the American people, were merely pawns in a global game of empire-building.

When the Defense Policy Guidance draft cowritten by Paul Wolfowitz and Scooter Libby was leaked to the *New York Times* in 1992, a horrified Senator Joseph Biden described it as a blueprint for "literally a Pax Americana." The document reflected the neoconservative vision for a "New American Century," a world defined by U.S. military domination over much of Europe and Asia, buttressed by a global ring of military bases, each ready to dispatch troops at the slightest hint of resistance from "hostile" states. It was time, neoconservatives argued, to take advantage of an unparalleled "unipolar moment" marked by the collapse of the Soviet Union.

While the Clinton administration viewed the post–Cold War era as an opportunity to create a series of multilateral alliances that would allow the U.S. to cut back on its military commitments, Dick Cheney's protégés saw a wide-open road to an American empire. With the Soviets out of the way, the United States could stride unrestrained across the international arena, using its vastly greater military and economic resources to shape the world to its will without any need for apologies or alliances.

Iraq, then, is merely the first "test case" for this radical foreign policy. The war was not fought for freedom, democracy, security, or even strictly for oil. Iraqi oil is important to the Bush administration, but in the sense that control of Middle Eastern oil is central to the neoconservative plan for U.S. supremacy. No country can hope to rule the world without controlling its access to oil. The lucrative contracts for U.S. oil companies were intended as the icing that would pay for the cake—i.e., the occupation of Iraq. As it turns out, while Halliburton did indeed turn its fortunes around thanks to the war, the Bush administration is running itself and the country into the red.

The unraveling of the administration's Iraq plan is symptomatic of inherent flaws in the Bush doctrine itself, which relies heavily on "hot preemption"—the use of direct military confrontation to eliminate any potential threats to U.S. interests or rivals to its primacy. Wars, however, are expensive. The Bush administration assumed that other nations under duress will subsidize the American empire—chipping in their money and their armies to avoid incurring Uncle Sam's wrath. It made a completely erroneous calculation: military plus economic clout equals unassailable power.

The pitfalls of this assumption were made painfully clear in the lead-up to the war. In order to gain international support to finance its military campaign, the Bush administration threatened recalcitrant countries with economic penalties. Poorer countries were told that their IMF loans would be in jeopardy, while wealthier nations like Germany were threatened with the withdrawal of American military bases—a loss that would have a significant impact on the local economy. Despite this direct exercise of its considerable power, the U.S. was only able to gather 45 countries in its "coalition of the unwilling"— most of whom did little to ease either the financial or military burden of the war or its aftermath.

Today, we stand more isolated in the world than ever and in more need of its help. Just this one war is costing American taxpayers nearly a billion dollars a week. The future costs of this war are not limited to the $87 billion that George Bush has asked for, but encompass the $500 billion budget deficit projected for 2003. And Iraq was supposed to be just the first in a series of confrontations with the "axis of evil." Nor has the military victory worked quite as the neoconservatives wanted. Islamic jihadis are not cowering in fear but eagerly streaming into Iraq to take on the U.S. military. Rather than an awe-inspiring superpower, the U.S. appears embattled and overwhelmed in the eyes of the world. In its very first excursion into reality, the great imperial plan devised by the neoconservatives has proved to be a resounding failure. Nor has there been the predicted positive domino effect in the region, especially in bringing peace to Israel through Bush's so-called "road map."

Contrary to the claims of the Bush administration, its policies over the past three years—be it on Iraq, the International Court of Justice, or the Kyoto Protocol—did not just prove the ability of the U.S. to take unilateral action. They also revealed the greater willingness of allies to break ranks with the last standing superpower. In a post–Cold War world, other countries may not be able to stop the U.S. from waging war, but they also no longer need to jump at its bidding. Yet, faced with unexpected resistance from the United Nations and many of its closest allies, the hawks did not rethink their plan but instead clung to the idea that an overwhelming victory would bring the rest of the world around. Of the five lies that we have laid out in this book, there is perhaps only one that the administration itself may have truly believed: Remaking Iraq would be "a cakewalk." But it was a delusion borne of greed and ideological hubris. Neoconservatives claimed to always know best—better than the vast array of foreign policy experts, historians, and experienced generals who pointed to the mountain of evidence to the contrary.

In sum, Iraq in 2003 is a microcosm of a plan based on delusion executed through a policy of calculated deception. Much of this book has been devoted to documenting the catastrophic results of these dangerous lies told in the service of this administration's imperial dream.

We Americans didn't really choose this road to self-destruction. We were led down the garden path, so to speak, having been filled with high-minded platitudes about our unique purpose in the world as defenders of all that is good and noble. Americans were told neither of the foolish designs for global supremacy nor the truth about Saddam Hussein. As a citizenry, we were misled to such a degree, on such an important matter, that it was nothing less than a clear subversion of the spirit and law of our democratic system. Now an entire nation has to pay the price for the overweening arrogance of a few men.

The costs of this war are not just a matter of mind-boggling budget deficits or a casualty counter that ticks steadily upward. It is not the $70-plus billion that this war has cost us at the time of writing of this book, or the additional $87 billion that Bush wants. The numbers don't reveal the threat this war poses to our livelihood, the welfare of our families, and the future of our children. According to CostOfWar.com, a website that measures this unhappy trade-off, we could have spent the same $70 billion to hire a million school teachers or provide health care for 24 million children for a year.

The Center for American Progress estimates that the $87 billion in additional funding is double what we spend on Homeland Security, 10 times what we spend on environmental protection, and 87 times what we spend on after-school programs. We are paying for this war as we face cutbacks to our local school systems, our ability to get adequate health insurance and care for our poor. So will our children pay. Analyzing the impact of authorizing the White House's request, the *New York Times* reported, "Administration officials acknowledged the next day that every dollar of the cost will be borrowed, a loan that economists say will be repaid by the next generation of taxpayers and the generation after that." The burden of the war grows heavier with each passing day.

Americans seem to be finally waking up to the enormity of the Faustian bargain they struck with this administration in the wake of the 9/11 attacks. Two years later, we have woken from our fear-induced trance and find ourselves both less safe and less free, betrayed by a president who asked us for our trust. A September poll conducted by the *Washington Post* showed that 61 percent of the American people opposed the president's plan to throw another $87 billion into the Iraqi quagmire. The president's own approval numbers are tumbling. And while most Americans still support the decision to go to war, 53 percent of respondents were "very concerned" about getting bogged down in Iraq, up from 41 percent in a poll taken three weeks earlier.

The ominous poll numbers, multiplying costs, and a steady procession of body bags appear to have forced the White House to amend its "my way or the highway" attitude. Bush's speech to the UN on Iraq in September 2003 was as close as he has come to an admission of failure: "I recognize that not all of our friends agreed with our decision" to invade and occupy Iraq, he magnanimously allowed. "Yet we cannot let past differences interfere with present duties." Translation: We once thought it was Europe and the United Nations' duty to shut up and get out of our way. Now we think it is their duty to hurry up and throw us a rope.

Perhaps the Security Council will indeed bail out the White House— though not on its terms. To share the burden it is most likely that the U.S. will have to transfer the political administration of Iraq over to the UN. As Ian Williams, UN correspondent for *The Nation,* put it, "It is time to bid a fond farewell to its grand schemes for long-term military bases, pipelines to Israel, or selling the shop at bargain-basement prices to Halliburton and Bechtel." At this time, there is still no sign that the Bush administration is willing to do any of the above. Faced with an opportunity to make a case for much-needed international assistance in his September 23 speech to the General Assembly, the president chose instead to display his trademark bluster. Slate.com's Fred Kaplan wrote, "Bush's message can be summarized as follows: The U.S.-led occupation authority is doing good work in Iraq; you should come help us; if you don't, you're on the side of the terrorists."

Even if the White House does see the light, an influx of international assistance may lighten our burden but will do little to repair the damage that has already been done. No one can bring back the hundreds of U.S. soldiers and countless Iraqis lost to the war. A change of course at this late stage will unlikely avert the financial crisis that looms in our future. We will have to reap the whirlwind sown by this president in one way or the other.

In the months to come, with the presidential elections around the corner, George Bush will no doubt do whatever it takes to try to maintain his grip on the presidency. But while the administration may adopt a minor course correction on Iraq, there is little hope for significant change. Make no mistake: Whatever the shift in rhetoric, their goals and strategy still remain the same. The 9/11 attacks are now more important than ever. According to *New York Times* columnist Paul Krugman, "It may be harder for the administration to wrap itself in the flag, but it has more incentive to do so now than ever before. Where once the administration was motivated by greed, now it's driven by fear." There will be little respite from the daily blitzkrieg of lies, evasions, and misinformation spewing out of the White House in the heat of the presidential battle.

It is no accident that the president seems incapable of speaking the truth to his people about this war. To stop lying to the American public the administration would have to stop lying to itself. To admit failure on Iraq is to bring into question its entire foreign policy. It would have to recognize the absurdity of its grandiose imperial plans, built on flimsy delusions of grandeur. It would have to acknowledge the wrong-headedness of an ideology that valorizes might over right. Krugman predicts, "The administration's infallibility complex—its inability to admit ever making a mistake—will get even worse. . . . In other words, if you thought the last two years were bad, just wait: It's about to get worse. A lot worse."

The lies detailed in this book are merely a symptom of a dangerous disease that afflicts the Bush administration. Neither the suffering of U.S. soldiers and Iraqi civilians nor a massive economic crisis will deflect its sense of entitlement. The only question that remains is how long Americans will continue to place their trust in these false messiahs who choose to play God with the fate of our nation and the world.

About the Authors and AlterNet

CHRISTOPHER SCHEER is a staff writer at AlterNet, the independent news and commentary website.

ROBERT SCHEER is the author of six books and is currently a clinical professor of communications at The Annenberg School at the University of Southern California. He is a nationally syndicated columnist based at the *Los Angeles Times,* a contributing editor at *The Nation,* and a host of NPR affiliate KCRW's *Left, Right, and Center.*

LAKSHMI CHAUDHRY is a senior editor at AlterNet.

ALTERNET (www.AlterNet.org) is an acclaimed Internet magazine and information source that provides readers with crucial facts and passionate opinions. Since its inception in 1997, AlterNet has grown dramatically to keep pace with the public demand for independent news and now provides free on-line content to more than 1.5 million visitors every month. "Special Coverage" sections report in depth on the war in Iraq, the environment, media and culture, civil liberties, and the drug war. AlterNet is a project of the Independent Media Institute—a nonprofit media company—that also includes AlterNet Syndication; WireTap Magazine (www.wiretapmag.org), an on-line magazine by and for socially conscious youth; and the Strategic Press Information Network (www.spinproject.org), a communications project that provides media trainings to grassroots and advocacy organizations to enhance the power of their message.

About the Publishers

AKASHIC BOOKS is an award-winning, Brooklyn-based independent company dedicated to publishing urban literary fiction and political non-fiction by authors who are either ignored by the mainstream, or who have no interest in working within the ever-consolidating ranks of the major corporate publishers. Akashic Books hosts additional imprints, including RDV Books, Dennis Cooper's Little House on the Bowery series, the Akashic Urban Surreal series, and the Akashic Cuban Noir series.

For more information, visit www.akashicbooks.com, email Akashic7@aol.com, or write us at Akashic Books, PO Box 1456, New York, NY 10009.

SEVEN STORIES PRESS is an independent book publisher based in New York City, with distribution throughout the United States, Canada, England, and Australia. Seven Stories publishes works of the imagination by such writers as Nelson Algren, Octavia E. Butler, Assia Djebar, Ariel Dorfman, Lee Stringer, and Kurt Vonnegut, to name a few, together with political titles by voices of conscience, including the Boston Women's Health Book Collective, Noam Chomsky, Ralph Nader, Gary Null, Project Censored, Barbara Seaman, Gary Webb, and Howard Zinn, among many others. Their books appear in hardcover, paperback, pamphlet, and e-book formats, in English and in Spanish. Seven Stories Press believes publishers have a special responsibility to defend free speech and human rights wherever they can.

For more information visit www.sevenstories.com or write for a free catalogue to Seven Stories Press, 140 Watts Street, New York, NY 10013.